CONTENTS

ILLUSTRATIONS

PREFACE

In October 1986 the first-ever national conference devoted solely to Canadian children's and young-adult literature (Canadian Images Canadiennes, sponsored by the Manitoba School Library Audio Visual Association) was held in Winnipeg and attracted nearly 500 delegates. An event of this magnitude could not have taken place ten years ago. It marked the coming of age of Canadian children's literature and the culmination of a decade of literary growth from 1975 to 1985.

Modern Canadian Children's Books is a survey of significant titles and developments in the genres of picture-books, fiction, the oral tradition, and poetry during that exciting decade. This overview focuses on literary rather than informational or dramatic works, therefore non-fiction and plays, whose development deserves separate critical attention, are not discussed. Bibliographical entries of Canadian works cited appear at the end of each chapter. All of these entries have been checked against *Canadiana* and *Canadian Books in Print 1986* (bound and microfiche update, October 1986), and Canadian publishers (or distributors) have been given wherever possible.

The creative surge of the last decade in the writing, illustration, and publishing of children's books in Canada has been paralleled by a substantial increase in criticism of the literature. I am most grateful for the insights and inspiration I have derived from this growing body of criticism. In particular, I wish to acknowledge my debt to Sheila Egoff's seminal *The Republic of Childhood: A Critical Guide to Canadian Children's Literature in English**, Sarah Ellis's 'News from

---

*Sheila Egoff, *The Republic of Childhood: A Critical Guide to Canadian Children's Literature in English*, 2d edn (Toronto, Oxford University Press, 1975).

the North' column in *The Horn Book Magazine*, and the many fine articles in *Canadian Children's Literature/Littérature canadienne pour la jeunesse: A Journal of Criticism and Review*.

Of further assistance to me were the ideas developed in discussion with students at the School of Library, Archival and Information Studies, University of British Columbia, and with friends and colleagues Sue Ann Alderson, William Barringer, Corinne Durston, Sheila Egoff, Sarah Ellis, and Kit Pearson. I would also like to thank William Toye and Patricia Sillers for their editorial guidance.

Finally, I am grateful to the International Board on Books for Young People (Canadian Section) for the research funding assistance of its Frances E. Russell Award.

1

THE WRITING AND PUBLISHING OF CANADIAN CHILDREN'S BOOKS

Nineteen seventy-five was a watershed year for the writing and publishing of Canadian children's books in English. The conservative, problem-laden years before the early 1970s—years of slow development in a struggling, insecure industry—gave way to the energetic decade (1975 to 1985) of creative and economic growth that has led to the distinctive national children's literature of the present day.

Before 1975 the difficulties of writing and publishing Canadian children's books seemed insurmountable and the literature's achievements modest and conservative. In the second edition of her *Republic of Childhood: A Critical Guide to Children's Literature in English* (1975), Sheila Egoff studied the historical roots, accomplishments, and lacunae of a still embryonic children's literature and concluded that its strengths were in the traditions of the outdoor adventure and survival story, the animal story, the novel of Canadian history, and the retellings of Indian and Inuit myths and legends; its weaknesses in genres such as the contemporary realistic novel, fantasy and science fiction, and non-fiction; and its seeds of promise in picture-books and poetry. Canadian children's literature was seen as immature, insular, and uneven; it was not yet a substantial body of writing nor international in literary quality, but it held the promise of continuing development.

PROBLEMS OF PUBLISHING CHILDREN'S BOOKS IN CANADA

But this forecast of gradual growth to maturity was threatened by the difficulties besetting the publishing industry—symbolized in 1970 by the sale of the financially troubled Ryerson Press, the influential Canadian publisher that had been founded in the 1890s, to an American firm. The problems were documented in reports by government commissions, such as the 1971 Ontario Royal Commission on Book Publishing, and in studies of the industry, such as the 1977 Secretary of State's *The Publishing Industry in Canada*. But when applied to children's books, the familiar difficulties plaguing the publishing of adult books in Canada in 1975 seemed multiplied beyond measure. Most of them still apply today. The market for Canadian children's books is composed of a small audience scattered across a vast distance and divided by language. Out of Canada's population of nearly 25 million, approximately 18 million are English-speaking; only 7 to 8 million of these are estimated to compose the book market, and of this category, a mere 3 to 6 million are considered the market for indigenous Canadian publishing. Obviously, only a small percentage of this last figure would be buyers of children's books. Book-buying, not only by the general public, but by public and school libraries, has been weak. Canada's immense territory makes distribution, promotion, and publicity erratic and expensive. The scant coverage of children's books in professional reviewing journals, general newspapers and magazines, and the mass media has meant that teachers, librarians, and the general public have had little opportunity to learn of new titles. And, since Canada is the largest book-importing country in the world, there is heavy competition from a massive flood of imported English-language children's books from British and American publishers with large home markets, print runs, and budgets, as well as from Canadian subsidiaries of foreign publishers subsidized by their parent houses. Books by Canadian authors account for only about twenty-six per cent of the trade purchases in Canadian bookstores. Besides these difficulties, there are few children's-book editors to supply editorial guidance and art direction.

Economics, however, still remains the main stumbling-block. Manufacturing costs, particularly for picture-books, which are capital-intensive, are about twenty per cent higher in Canada than in the United States or Britain, and there are no economies of scale in Canadian publishing to lower the cost per book. The small size of the Canadian book market limits the average print run of a Canadian children's book to approximately 5,000 copies, forcing the unit cost of children's books—many of which are illustrated and therefore more than usually expensive to produce—to be extremely high (exorbitant in the eyes of many book buyers) in comparison with that of American children's books, which, because of the enormous American population and market, can be printed in larger runs at a lower unit price and with greater profits. In the past, this disincentive was compounded for publishers by the lack of a substantial backlist of Canadian children's standards or classics to underwrite financial investment in new authors and publishing ventures.

Publishers in the early 1970s complained of a dearth of first-rate manuscripts, talented writers, and illustrators. The literature was littered with one- and two-book writers who had abandoned the field. This was not surprising. Without guidance from professional children's editors, there were few opportunities for writers and illustrators to learn their craft. And, to make the situation even more discouraging, Canadian writers for children were eligible for fewer grants than were writers for adults and illustrators routinely earned less on a book than writers and were eligible for even fewer government grants.

In the light of these harsh realities, only a few of the large, general trade publishing houses, such as McClelland and Stewart, Macmillan, and Oxford Canada, devoted editorial energy and financial commitment to producing a children's list. The volume was infinitesimal: only thirty to forty children's books published annually through the 1950s and 1960s.

In such a climate it was inevitable that most of the books offered to children were classic and popular British and American titles—a reflection of the colonial mentality that considered non-Canadian writing a more valuable literary heritage than indigenous writing for children.

In this gloomy context the unprecedented growth in one short decade from a frail to an almost robust industry and to a literature that, at its best, can compete internationally seems very dramatic and sudden.

GROWTH AND EXPANSION IN PUBLISHING

The maturing of the Canadian children's-book industry resulted from many influences, including those that mirrored great changes in other segments of society. One major impetus was the rising Canadian nationalism of the late sixties and early seventies. In the late 1960s and early 1970s small presses emerged—cultural nationalists such as House of Anansi, Oberon, and James Lorimer— that were devoted to indigenous adult Canadian writing and were assisted by increased government subsidies from the Canada Council and provincial arts councils. This trend was paralleled in children's publishing by the rise of small, alternative presses for children's books (often begun as federally funded Opportunities for Youth and Local Initiatives projects and often funded as non-profit collectives, such as The Women's Press and Kids Can Press, both in Toronto). Devoted to child advocacy, the exploration of nationalist issues, and non-sexism and multiculturalism, the inexpensive, amateurishly produced children's books published by these houses in their early years tended to express strong, often admirable, social convictions in didactic or dull stories. In the same period, however, an innovative Montreal publishing house, Tundra Books, pioneered Canadian children's picture-books as works of art, establishing high standards and winning numerous awards, both at home and on the international scene. In the later 1960s and early 1970s the publications of the socially minded alternative presses and of the aesthetically minded art houses joined the small body of good children's books already being produced by the commercial houses to foster an atmosphere of growth.

In the mid-1970s a roster of 'firsts' drew attention to the Canadian children's-literature scene and generated publishing momentum. In 1974 the Children's Book Store opened in Toronto. Now internationally known, it has been joined in the last decade by approximately forty specialized, independent children's bookstores across the country. A new market for Canadian children's books was created by the baby-boom generation who were lavishing educational and recreational care upon their children. The first generation to have studied adult Canadian literature in schools, colleges, and universities, these parents now supported both Canadian children's books and the Canadian children's record industry. Parents and other concerned adults came to realize that only a small number of books were available to Canadian children that significantly reflected images of Canadian life and what it is like to be Canadian—books informed by the sensibility of home. As people were exposed to more and better Canadian children's books they began to see that such books could be instrumental in transmitting the nation's political, social, and imaginative culture, thereby giving children an awareness of Canada's physical and emotional geography and history. A sense of heritage and identity could be nurtured if children encountered, in their reading, their own personal world, validated by the power of the imagination. Children's literature was viewed as a potentially unifying force that could transcend the country's fragmentary regionalism and vast scale giving shape to local experience and helping to foster a national culture.

In 1975 and 1976 the first international children's literature conferences in Canada were held in Toronto (the 8th Loughborough International Summer Seminar on Children's Literature) and in Vancouver (the Pacific Rim Conference on Children's Literature). Children's literature was finally considered worthy of academic study. 1975 also saw the founding of the first journal devoted to serious criticism of our national juvenile literature: *Canadian Children's Literature/Littérature canadienne pour la jeunesse*. Despite the serious blow, in 1982, of the demise of *In Review*, the major Canadian reviewing journal for children's books, there has been a slow improvement in the spotty coverage of Canadian children's books. In addition to reviews and articles in national book trade, reviewing, and literary journals, such as *Books in Canada*, *CM: Canadian Materials*, and *Quill & Quire*, there has been a slight increase in attention from general magazines and newspapers and the electronic media: for example, in the children's-book column in the *Globe and Mail* and the children's-book panel on the CBC radio program 'Morningside'. But the mandate of the *Children's Book News* is promotional rather than critical, and *Emergency Librarian*, despite its reviews of some professional publications and children's paperbacks, is not a reviewing journal. In such international journals as *The Horn Book Magazine* and the *Children's Literature Association Quarterly*, some space is devoted to columns on Canadian children's books, but there is still no journal that supplies the comprehensive and comparative reviewing necessary to evaluate Canadian children's books in the context of international children's literature.

With the establishment of the Canada Council Children's Literature Prizes in 1976, the number of national literary awards and prizes that stimulate sales and draw the media's attention to children's books has grown from the two Canadian Association of Children's Librarians

Awards for art and text offered before 1975 to over ten separate national and several regional awards. Also, in 1976 the National Library of Canada established a position of Children's Literature Librarian, which has evolved into a national children's literature service with professional functions that benefit the country's libraries and publishing industry. Over the last decade there has been an evident increase in support from the previously hesitant institutional market of public and school libraries.

Other agencies devoted to Canadian children's-book promotion were also founded at this time. In 1976 the Children's Book Centre in Toronto (along with its French-Canadian counterpart, Communication-Jeunesse, founded in 1971) began to function as a promotional organization and information clearing-house. In 1977 the centre inaugurated the annual Children's Book Festival, which, along with the Canada Council National Book Festival and an increase in tours and readings by authors, has raised the literature's profile and augmented the meagre income of Canadian writers and illustrators.

This burgeoning interest in children's books was partially stimulated by a single publishing success story—the publication of Dennis Lee's best-selling collection of Canadian nonsense verse, *Alligator Pie*, in 1974. Its phenomenal sales and critical and popular accalim showed publishers that there was more financial incentive in children's-book publishing than they had expected. Larger houses expanded their children's lists, and the number of small-press children's publishers increased. A small number of children's-book editors added their knowledge to the field. Within a decade several of the independent alternative publishers had matured beyond their polemical roots to create higher-quality publications with improved physical production and a broader, non-sectarian appeal. Regional publishers, such as Tree Frog Press in Edmonton, flourished. And eventually there developed a core of firms committed to publishing only children's books. Although many large publishers bring out the occasional fine children's book, this tiny core of less than ten small houses is really responsible for the increased volume in children's publishing. Publishers diversified to specialize in particular genres: the non-fiction of Greey de Pencier and Kids Can Press; the young-adult novels of Groundwood Books and Irwin Publishing; the picture-books of Tundra Books and Annick Press, which, in 1984, set a precedent as the first-ever children's-book publisher to be honoured as 'Publisher of the Year' by the Canadian Booksellers Association.

Although the economics remains discouraging and the publishers continue to battle against great odds, the publishing industry is not only surviving, but, in many areas, expanding. This is partly due to more efficient distribution, more aggressive marketing and promotion, the building of modest backlists, and a search for other solutions to publishing problems. Publishers have come to realize that survival depends on publishing for the international as well as the domestic market. Since the late 1970s many publishers have followed the leadership of Tundra Books and Annick Press in establishing high profiles at international book fairs, such as the Bologna Children's Book Fair and the Frankfurt Book Fair. Canadian children's publishers, especially of picture-books, which are more readily exported than novels, are now representing their literature with confidence and seeking opportunities for international co-publication of first editions and reprints and for increased foreign-rights sales. This results in greatly enlarged print runs, generally of 15,000 to 25,000 (although sometimes up to 100,000 for mass-market sales), lower expenses and prices, increased publicity, and international recognition. The presses have also increased their purchases of Canadian rights to foreign books.

From 1975 to 1985 the increase in the number of children's authors and illustrators, and of titles and publishers, has been prodigious. The last decade witnessed a striking improvement in the quality of the books as physical objects and an increase in the diversity of genre, content, format, illustrative design, and literary theme. The change in the volume of publishing is impressive, rising from 30 or 40 books published annually during the 1950s and 1960s, through 416 between 1973 and 1977, to 150 to 200 in 1985. Committed writers and illustrators were no longer abandoning the field after one or two books but were staying to build the foundations of a substantial body of Canadian children's books—many of which could truly be called literature. It has been shown in publishing that the larger the volume of books written and published, the more opportunity there will be for a first-class literature to develop and for outstanding talents to surface. Now that the number of Canadian children's books published has multiplied, that axiom appears to be true. Considering the relatively modest number of Canadian titles published annually, and the fact that the literature is still distinctly uneven in quality, the standard of excellence is gradually rising in proportion to the best of the five to six thousand English-language children's books published elsewhere in the world. The best Canadian titles show an integrity, vitality, stylistic versatility, and, in many cases, a particular cultural voice and uniquely Canadian vision that render them significant and memorable. Canadian children's books are certainly travelling: they are being sold for foreign rights and co-publication, translated into other languages, and read by non-Canadians. Publishers and commentators appear to disagree on whether Canadian content is a liability or an advantage in selling outside Canada, on whether it is seen as parochial, exotic, or universal. But at home the books make their own way, despite some residual feeling that Canadian cultural works are inferior or second-rate.

A brief examination of the historical development of the literature will illustrate the cultural motifs, themes, and trends that contemporary children's books share with those of the past.

THE HISTORICAL DEVELOPMENT OF CANADIAN CHILDREN'S BOOKS

The first children's books of the Victorian period that may be called Canadian were written by visitors to Canada, temporary residents, or new immigrants and were more likely to be published in London, Boston, or New York than in Canada. The powerful Canadian landscape—the dangers, challenges, and awesome beauty of the wilderness and its wildlife—provided a dramatic backdrop and rich source of colourful incident for the classic Robinsonnade survival sagas, historical romances of exploration and the fur trade, and traditional boys' outdoor adventure stories of the time. Canadian settings and subjects appeared in Catherine Parr Traill's *Canadian Crusoes: A Tale of the Rice Lake Plains* (1852), which combined adventure with Christian moralizing, and R.M. Ballantyne's gripping narratives, such as *Snowflakes and Sunbeams; or The Young Fur Traders* (1856). Boys' adventure and school stories with an emphasis on Canadian outdoor life and with elements of didacticism continued into the twentieth century in the works of such Canadian-born writers as James de Mille, James MacDonald Oxley, Egerton Ryerson Young, and Norman Duncan.

The most talented writer in this genre was Ernest Thompson Seton, whose *Two Little Savages: Being the Adventures of Two Boys Who Lived as Indians and What They Learned* (1903) reveals the same strengths of vivid story-telling, sound natural history, and woodcraft lore—with the bonus of his own effective line drawings—that appear in his wild-animal biographies. The distinctive Canadian contribution to the animal story began with Marshall Saunders's sentimental and immensely popular dog story, *Beautiful Joe: An Autobiography* (1894). An entirely different, original, and more realistic approach to fictionalized animal stories was developed by Ernest Thompson Seton and Charles G.D. Roberts. Incorporating details made possible by a close observation of nature and first-hand knowledge of wild-animal behaviour, Seton's straightforward narratives, such as *Wild Animals I Have Known* (1898), and Roberts's more poetic tales, such as *The Kindred of the Wild* (1902), established the new Canadian genre of the realistic wild-animal biography.

The Edwardian tradition of domestic realism was explored in the sentimental school stories and moralistic child-and-family-life accounts of Ralph Connor's *Glengarry Schooldays* (1902) and Nellie McClung's *Sowing Seeds in Danny* (1908). This genre acquired a distinctive local Canadian voice in L.M. Montgomery's *Anne of Green Gables* (1908). The fresh originality of Anne's character, her boisterous sense of humour, emotional energy, wry observations of adult society and manners, and loving descriptions of Prince Edward Island made this book a Canadian classic and an international bestseller.

Few twentieth-century Canadian writers for children have received the international acclaim and popular acceptance of Seton, Roberts, or Montgomery, whose works dominated the first half of the century, when very little Canadian work was written and published for children and even less was memorable. However, it is possible to sift through much literary mediocrity and discover a body of strong, individual talents who successfully produced, in the years before 1975, children's books of some lasting merit, usually written in the established Canadian traditions. Both Roderick L. Haig-Brown (*Starbuck Valley Winter*, 1943) and Farley Mowat (*Lost in the Barrens*, 1956) combined the dramatic narrative elements of the outdoor-adventure story with the new theme of conservation presented with the exactitude of a naturalist's observant eye.

Both writers also worked in the tradition of the animal story. Haig-Brown's rather dry but accurate *Silver: The Life of an Atlantic Salmon* (1931) and *Ki-Yu: A Story of Panthers* (1934) contrast with Mowat's warm and humorous tales of children and pets in *The Dog Who Wouldn't Be* (1957) and *Owls in the Family* (1961). Among the other major works in this genre are Grey Owl's *The Adventures of Sajo and Her Beaver People* (1935), Sheila Burnford's *The Incredible Journey* (1960), and Cameron Langford's *The Winter of the Fisher* (1971).

Native Indian and Inuit life and lore have also been important subjects of Canadian children's books. Whether the form of expression is the rites-of-passage novels of West Coast Indian historical fiction (as in Edith Lambert Sharp's *Nkwala*, 1958, or Haig-Brown's *The Whale People*, 1962) or the timeless Inuit adventure and survival legends of James Houston, such as *Tikta'liktak* (1965) and *The White Archer* (1967), the anthropological accuracy and the sheer drama are thoroughly convincing and compelling.

A balance of cultural authenticity, interpretation, and literary shaping was also sought by the retellers of Indian and Inuit myths and legends. The collections ranged widely in tone, style, and content from the early works by Pauline Johnson (*Legends of Vancouver*, 1911) and Cyrus Macmillan (the European-styled *Canadian Wonder Tales*, 1918 and *Canadian Fairy Tales*, 1922) to the active group of retellers in the 1960s who sought a suitable form and style in which to make the multiform aboriginal legends more comprehensible to non-natives. Works of particular cohesion and impact are Robert Ayre's *Sketco the Raven* (1961), Christie Harris's *Once Upon a Totem* (1963), Kathleen Hill's *Glooscap and His Magic: Legends of the Wabanaki Indians* (1963), Dorothy Reid's *Tales of Nanabozho* (1963), and Ronald Melzack's *The Day Tuk Became a Hunter and Other Eskimo Stories* (1967). Native retellers, such as George Clutesi in *Son of Raven, Son of Deer: Fables of the Tse-Shaht People* (1967), began to collect and interpret tales from the still-living oral tradition of their people, stressing the continuity and timelessness of native lore and experience.

The Canadian oral tradition was also represented by collections of the rich French-Canadian folklore, as in Marius Barbeau's *The Golden*

Phoenix and Other French-Canadian Fairy Tales (1958), translated and adapted by Michael Hornyansky, and in Edith Fowke's anthology of Canada's oral child lore—the songs, rhymes, games, and street lore that children transmit in their own subculture—in *Sally Go Round the Sun: 300 Songs, Rhymes, and Games of Canadian Children* (1969).

In the range of fiction beyond the outdoor adventure story, realistic fiction and fantasy developed slowly in the years before 1975. Very few Canadian realistic family stories evolved in the direction of the new American social realism, the urban-problem novel of sociological and psychological turbulence that dominated international children's publishing in the 1960s and 1970s. Jean Little's stories of disabled children, such as *From Anna* (1972), have a more traditional domestic tone detailing episodic incidents of family relationships, friendships, and school experiences. Set in Toronto during the Second World War, some of Little's novels may be termed historical fiction of the recent past. The large number of historical-fiction writers who focus on major events of Canadian history in the more distant past have, on the whole, made rather lacklustre attempts to combine factual documentation with dramatic conflict and colourful characterization. *Flaming Prairie* (1965), which treats the Northwest Rebellion of 1885, and other works by John Hayes, and *Honor Bound* (1971), the adventures of a Loyalist family, by Mary Alice and John Downie, are representative of the genre.

Fantasy also remained a minor category in the years preceding 1975. Except for indigenous native legends, there is no substantial tradition in Canada of the magical and fabulous, no imaginative storehouse of themes and motifs drawn from folklore and mythology. This has hindered the growth of local fantasists, although there are notable exceptions, including Catherine Anthony Clark, whose magical stories, such as *The Golden Pine Cone* (1950), incorporate elements of the awesome British Columbia landscape and Indian spiritualism. A more classical fantasist is Ruth Nichols. Her traditional *A Walk Out of the World* (1969) and *The Marrow of the World* (1972) integrate Canadian settings with the quest structure and the symbolic conflict between good and evil found in the epic high fantasies of C.S. Lewis and J.R.R. Tolkien.

Before 1975 informational books concentrated on history and biography, with some educational and trade series attaining considerable quantity, if not often quality, in the treatment of Canadian figures and events. Only a few titles achieved any depth of feeling or serious engagement with Canada's past: Pierre Berton's *The Golden Trail: The Story of the Klondike Rush* (1954) and William Toye's *The St Lawrence* (1959) evoked the realities of Canadian history and geography in stimulating, thought-provoking presentations of authentic fact and specific, concrete detail.

Even fewer were the creators of poetry and picture-books. Unique in the field of children's verse, Dennis Lee's breakthrough bestseller *Alligator Pie* (1974) proved that it was possible to create a Canadian body of nursery rhymes, nonsense verse, and domestic poetry for young children. The skilfully selected anthology *The Wind Has Wings: Poems from Canada* (1968), edited by Mary Alice Downie and Barbara Robertson, mined the indigenous ore of Canadian adult poetry for works of appeal to children. It also ushered in a new era of memorable illustration in Canadian children's books as the first book of four-colour illustrations printed and published in Canada. Its collage illustrator, Elizabeth Cleaver, went on to produce a series of striking picture-books in collaboration with William Toye—single illustrated Indian legends, beginning with *The Mountain Goats of Temlaham* (1969).

The distressing paucity of Canadian picture-books was somewhat alleviated by the appearance of a group of longer picture-storybooks addressing themes of history and autobiography for young readers beyond pre-school age. One of the best was William Toye's *Cartier Discovers the St Lawrence* (1970), which evokes, through Laszlo Gal's handsome illustrations, the expanses of landscape and the suspenseful discovery of a new world. An important innovation in picture-book publishing has been a series of autobiographical memoirs of childhood experiences in the Canadian multicultural mosaic that documents regional cultures rising out of a particular place, time, and ethnic group. The texts are extended emotionally through pictorial story-telling in such works as Shizuye Takashima's reminiscences of Japanese-Canadian internment during the Second World War, *A Child in Prison Camp* (1971), and William Kurelek's memoirs of the Ukrainian-Canadian Depression era, *A Prairie Boy's Winter* (1973).

By 1975, despite the rudimentary level of achievement in many areas of the literature, there did exist a small nucleus of books worthy of consideration as the basis of a national children's literature. As well, the potential of the new authors and illustrators held definite promise for future growth.

That promise certainly was fulfilled between 1975 and 1985. From the evolving new literature of the past decade have emerged some noticeable thematic trends and narrative patterns. The traditional male outdoor-adventure story has persisted, but it has been altered to include female protagonists and has shifted the focus from physical survival to a more symbolic, psychological struggle in the wilderness leading to an integration of the self. Native and non-native retellers of indigenous traditional literature have begun to write with the inflections and personalized idioms of the oral story-teller's voice. An extension of the oral tradition now includes more non-native collections culled from the folklore and local legends of Canadian pioneers, settlers, immigrants, and ethnic groups. Some of these collections illustrate the process of acculturation: the impact of the new environment and the immigrant experience alters traditional stories from the homeland to create a new oral lore.

Although realistic fiction is still predominantly rural in setting, there has been a marked increase in the previously ignored genre of urban realism; many novels now interpret the inner emotional states and social realities of the vast majority of contemporary Canadian children's daily lives. There now exists the sparse beginning of a young-adult literature, which portrays Canadian adolescents' search for identity and coming of age within the context of contemporary social realism. In novels for both children and young adults one hears a chorus of recognizable voices articulating the multicultural and regional cadences of a pluralistic society. Historical fiction has evolved beyond large-scale historical romance to examine the minutiae of social theory in experiences such as immigration; the adjustment to a new country; the position of women in Canadian society; and racial, ethnic, class, or labour conflict. The writing of fantasy in Canada is exploring new forms, previously neglected, such as time-travel and science fiction, which, moving backwards into the past or forward into the future, emphasize human continuity in the face of political change or socio-cultural dissolution.

The burgeoning picture-book genre balances sophisticated works of elegant graphic design and fine art with those that are more child-centred. Poetry and plays have both enjoyed a resurgence of activity, represented by the emergence of new poets, an outpouring of single illustrated poems, and a flood of published scripts created by professional theatre companies for young people. A dramatic revival of informational books, apart from the traditional history and biography, extends the range of non-fiction to the arts and sciences. Other advances include the founding of children's magazines (e.g., *OWL* and *Chickadee*); the involvement of publishers in the production of television programs for children (e.g., OWL/TV); forays into mass-market lines (e.g., OWL Magazine/Golden Press Books); and experiments with unusual formats (e.g., Annikins). Also observable is a slight increase in bilingual texts and translations of children's books between English and French.

As a whole, the literary quality is still inconsistent and uneven. All genres have room for improvement and growth and individual works could be strengthened by more conscientious and rigorous editing to help writers develop their potential. There are pronounced gaps in certain categories, including picture-books, books for beginning readers, novels for the intermediate reader and young adult, all areas and age levels of non-fiction, especially history and biography, genres such as fantasy and science fiction, and translation between the two official languages. And one hopes that the didactic, polemical tone endemic to many of the treatments of historical incident and contemporary social causes will become less pronounced. The complexities of Canada's past and present deserve to be explored more sensitively in stories of deep emotional conviction written with narrative authority, rather than diminished by the sincere but mistaken belief that fiction is meant to serve didactic purposes.

Subsequent chapters will focus primarily on books that have achieved literary excellence. Each chapter will examine by genre the significant contributions to Canadian children's literature of the last decade: the major authors, illustrators, titles, and trends in picture-books, fiction, the oral tradition, and poetry that stand as landmarks on the map of our cultural imagination.

AYRE, ROBERT. *Sketco the Raven*. Illustrated by Philip Surrey. Toronto, Macmillan, 1961, cloth (O.P.)

BALLANTYNE, R.M. *Snowflakes and Sunbeams; or, The Young Fur Traders: A Tale of the Far North*. London, Nelson, 1856, cloth (O.P.)

BARBEAU, MARIUS. *The Golden Phoenix, and Other French-Canadian Fairy Tales*. Retold by Michael Hornyansky. Illustrated by Arthur Price. Toronto, Oxford, 1958, cloth (O.P.); Reprinted under title: *The Golden Phoenix, and Other Fairy Tales from Quebec*. 1980, paper.

BERTON, PIERRE. *The Golden Trail: The Story of the Klondike Rush*. Illustrated by Duncan Macpherson. Toronto, Macmillan, 1954, cloth (Great Stories of Canada) (O.P.); Richmond Hill, Ont., Scholastic-TAB, 1985, paper.

BURNFORD, SHEILA. *The Incredible Journey: A Tale of Three Animals*. Illustrated by Carl Burger. Boston/Toronto, Little, 1960, cloth (O.P.)

Chickadee: The Magazine for Young Children. Toronto, The Young Naturalist Foundation, 1979-.

CLARK, CATHERINE ANTHONY. *The Golden Pine Cone*. Illustrated by Clare Bice. Toronto, Macmillan, 1950, cloth (O.P.)

CLUTESI, GEORGE. *Son of Raven, Son of Deer: Fables of the Tse-Shaht People*. Illustrated by the author. Sidney, B.C., Gray's, 1967, cloth (O.P.); 1975, paper.

CONNOR, RALPH, pseud. (Charles W. Gordon). *Glengarry Schooldays: A Story of Early Days in Glengarry*. Chicago, Revell, 1902, cloth (O.P.); Toronto, M & S, 1975, paper (New Canadian Library)

DOWNIE, MARY ALICE AND JOHN DOWNIE. *Honor Bound*. Illustrated by Joan Huffman. Toronto, Oxford, 1971, cloth (O.P.); 1980, paper.

DOWNIE, MARY ALICE AND BARBARA ROBERTSON, comps. *The Wind Has Wings: Poems from Canada*. Illustrated by Elizabeth Cleaver. Toronto, Oxford, 1968, cloth (O.P.); 1978, paper (O.P.); Rev. edn under title: *The New Wind Has Wings: Poems from Canada*. 1984, cloth, paper.

FOWKE, EDITH. *Sally Go Round the Sun: 300 Songs, Rhymes, and Games of Canadian Children*. Musical arrangements by Keith MacMillan. Illustrated by Carlos Marchiori. Designed by Frank Newfeld and Don Fernley. Toronto/Montreal, M & S, 1969, cloth.

GREY OWL, pseud. (Archibald Stansfeld Belaney). *The Adventures of Sajo and Her Beaver People*. Toronto, Macmillan, 1935, cloth (O.P.); Reprinted under title: *Sajo and the Beaver People*. 1977, paper (Laurentian Library)

HAIG-BROWN, RODERICK L. *Ki-Yu: A Story of Panthers*. Illustrated by Theyre Lee-Elliott. Boston, Houghton, 1934, cloth (O.P.).

_____. *Silver: The Life of an Atlantic Salmon*. Illustrated by J.P. Moreton. London, Black, 1931, cloth (O.P.)

_____. *Starbuck Valley Winter*. Toronto, M & S, 1943, cloth (O.P.)

_____. *The Whale People*. Illustrated by Mary Weiler. London, Collins, 1962, cloth (O.P.); Toronto, Totem, 1982, paper.

HARRIS, CHRISTIE. *Once Upon a Totem*. Woodcuts by John Frazer Mills. Toronto, M & S, 1963, cloth (O.P.); 1978, paper (Canadian Favourites)

HAYES, JOHN F. *Flaming Prairie: A Story of the Northwest Rebellion of 1885*. Illustrated by Fred J. Finley. Vancouver, Copp, 1965, cloth (O.P.)

HILL, KATHLEEN L. *Glooscap and His Magic: Legends of the Wabanaki Indians*. Illustrated by Robert Frankenberg. Toronto, M & S, 1963, cloth (O.P.); 1973, paper (Canadian Favourites)

HOUSTON, JAMES. *Tikta'liktak: An Eskimo Legend*. Illustrated by the author. Don Mills, Ont., Longmans, 1965, cloth (O.P.)

_____ *The White Archer: An Eskimo Legend*. Illustrated by the author. Don Mills, Ont., Longmans, 1967, cloth (O.P.)

JOHNSON, EMILY PAULINE. *Legends of Vancouver*. Illustrated by Ben Lim. New edn Toronto, M & S, 1961, paper. (Originally published in 1911 in a privately printed edition.)

KURELEK, WILLIAM. *A Prairie Boy's Winter*. Illustrated by the author. Montreal, Tundra, 1973, cloth; 1984, paper.

LANGFORD, CAMERON. *The Winter of the Fisher*. Toronto, Macmillan, 1971, cloth (O.P.); 1985, paper (Laurentian Library)

LEE, DENNIS. *Alligator Pie*. Pictures by Frank Newfeld. Toronto, Macmillan, 1974, cloth.

LITTLE, JEAN. *From Anna*. Pictures by Joan Sandin. Toronto, Fitzhenry, 1972, cloth (O.P.); 2nd edn, 1977, paper (The Contemporary Scene)

McCLUNG, NELLIE L. *Sowing Seeds in Danny*. New York, Doubleday, 1908, cloth (O.P.)

MACMILLAN, CYRUS. *Canadian Fairy Tales*. Illustrated by Marcia Lane Foster. London, Lane, 1922, cloth (O.P.)

_____. *Canadian Wonder Tales*. Illustrated by George Sheringham. London, Lane, 1918, cloth (O.P.); Reissued, with *Canadian Fairy Tales*, under title: *Canadian Wonder Tales*. Illustrated by Elizabeth Cleaver. Toronto, Clarke, 1974, cloth (O.P.)

MELZACK, RONALD. *The Day Tuk Became a Hunter and Other Eskimo Stories*. Illustrated by Carol Jones. Toronto, M & S, 1967, cloth (O.P.); 1978, paper.

MONTGOMERY, LUCY MAUD. *Anne of Green Gables*. Boston, Page, 1908, cloth (O.P.); Toronto, McGraw, 1942, cloth; McGraw, 1968, paper; Toronto, Seal, 1976, paper.

MOWAT, FARLEY M. *The Dog Who Wouldn't Be*. Illustrated by Paul Galdone. Boston/Toronto, Little, 1957, cloth (O.P.); Toronto, Seal, 1980, paper.

_____. *Lost in the Barrens*. Illustrated by Charles Geer. Boston/Toronto, Little, 1956, cloth (O.P.); Toronto, M & S, 1973, educ. edn, paper, collector's edn.

_____. *Owls in the Family*. Illustrated by Robert Frankenberg. Boston/Toronto, Little, 1961, cloth (O.P.); Toronto, M & S, 1973, paper; M & S, 1980, Collector's edn.

NICHOLS, RUTH. *The Marrow of the World*. Illustrated by Trina Schart Hyman. Toronto, Macmillan, 1972, cloth (O.P.); Toronto, Gage, 1977, educ. edn paper.

_____. *A Walk Out of the World*. Illustrated by Trina Schart Hyman. Toronto, Academic, 1969, cloth.

OWL: The Discovery Magazine for Children. Toronto, Young Naturalist Foundation, 1976-.

REID, DOROTHY M. *Tales of Nanabozho*. Illustrated by Donald Grant. Toronto, Oxford, 1963, cloth (O.P.)

ROBERTS, CHARLES G.D. *The Kindred of the Wild: A Book of Animal Life*. Illustrated by Charles Livingston Bull. Boston, Page, 1902, cloth (O.P.)

SAUNDERS, MARGARET MARSHALL. *Beautiful Joe: An Autobiography*. Philadelphia, American Baptist, 1894, cloth (O.P.); Toronto, M & S, 1972, paper (Canadian Favourites); M & S, 1985, paper.

SETON, ERNEST THOMPSON. *Two Little Savages: Being the Adventures of Two Boys Who Lived as Indians and What They Learned*. Illustrated by the author. New York, Grosset, 1903, cloth (O.P.)

_____. *Wild Animals I Have Known: Being the Personal Histories of Lobo, Silverspot, Raggylug, Bingo, The Springfield Fox, The Pacing Mustang, Wully and Redruff*. Illustrated by the author. New York, Scribner, 1898, cloth (O.P.); Toronto, M & S, 1977, paper (New Canadian Library)

SHARP, EDITH LAMBERT. *Nkwala*. Illustrated by William Winter. Boston/Toronto, Little, 1958, cloth (O.P.); Toronto, M & S, 1974, paper (Canadian Favourites)

TAKASHIMA, SHIZUYE. *A Child in Prison Camp*. Illustrated by the author. Montreal, Tundra, 1971, cloth; 1983, paper.

TOYE, WILLIAM. *Cartier Discovers the St Lawrence*. Illustrated by Laszlo Gal. Toronto, Oxford, 1970, cloth (O.P.); 1979, paper.

_____. *The St Lawrence*. Illustrated by Leo Rampen. Toronto, Oxford, 1959, cloth (O.P.)

_____. *The Mountain Goats of Temlaham*. Pictures by Elizabeth Cleaver. Toronto, Oxford, 1969, cloth (O.P.), paper.

TRAILL, CATHARINE PARR (Strickland). *Canadian Crusoes: A Tale of the Rice Lake Plains*. London, Hall, 1852, cloth (O.P.); Ottawa, Carleton University, 1986, cloth, paper (Early Canadian Texts)

2

PICTURE-BOOKS
AND PICTURE-STORYBOOKS

The picture-book is often a microcosm of a country's literature for children, reflecting in miniature the nation's themes and cultural vision. Because the picture-book is a condensed literary and artistic genre, form and content are more concentrated and immediate than in the broader genres of fiction and non-fiction; the perceptions of individual authors and illustrators are naturally distilled to a personal or cultural essence. The picture-book portrays in bold relief the themes of a specific Canadian literature for children. Stripped of the complexities, ambiguities, and plethora of detail involved in developing fuller characterization, plot, and setting for an older reader, the picture-book is condensed to a bright kernel of experience.

And because the picture-book weds art and text into an indivisible whole, it offers a new dimension of expression for the Canadian experience: visual images united with words. In Canadian picture-books the illustrations often extend the text both narratively and emotionally to evoke and depict a Canadian sensibility beyond what may be conveyed in even the most complex of novels. Although the language of pictures is international and universal (unlike the many languages of the written word), it reaches the universal through the particular. Babar and Peter Rabbit speak a universal language, but they also speak worlds about French and English culture respectively. In a wordless absorption, children experience through picture-books (in a way no number of words could convey) both the concrete sense of place and the less tangible sense of meaning of a specific culture.

Canadian picture-books convey the impact of a regional culture and milieu as often as they evoke Canada as a whole. While the emphasis on the visual image does not devalue the power of the text, which is crucial, the visual image is more immediately connected with rendering the wonder of being in the world, the emotional connection of physicality—the sense of our particular place, our specific home, in the here and now.

HISTORICAL DEVELOPMENT OF PICTURE-BOOKS IN CANADA

The picture-book genre is the fastest-growing, most aggressively marketed, and most vital sector of the industry in Canada today. This was not always the case. The picture-book, now the Cinderella success story of Canadian children's literature, was the slowest of all genres to develop from its dismal beginnings as the poor step-child of the industry—labouring in the cinders without beauty, love, or recognition. Until the early 1970s few Canadian publishers brought out picture-books of any merit. For the most part, what did exist was decidedly insignificant. On the whole, picture-books were poorly produced, limited to black and white or monochromatic illustrations, and uninspired in design, execution, and theme. A severe problem was the shortage of affordable expertise in the complex printing processes that are required to produce full-colour picture-books. Canadian picture-books appeared sporadically from the 1930s on, and some major publishers, such as Oxford Canada, produced the occasional high-quality picture-book in the 1960s focusing on the Canadian experience, such as Frank Newfeld's illustrated French-Canadian folktale, *The Princess of Tomboso* (1960), and the first of William Toye's and Elizabeth Cleaver's collaborative series of single illustrated Indian legends, *The Mountain Goats of Temlaham* (1969) and *How Summer Came to Canada* (1969). But it was not until the early 1970s that the emerging new wave of Canadian picture-books became a noticeable phenomenon.

The years from 1975 to 1985 saw a transformation in the publishing of Canadian picture-books and in the books themselves, partly as a result of the use of Hong Kong colour printing, which was cheaper than that in Canada. There was also an explosion in the range of visual style, energy of expression, and diversity of content and format. This change had its roots in the earlier ground-breaking work of a few picture-book creators: Elizabeth Cleaver, Ann Blades, Laszlo Gal, and Frank Newfeld were harbingers of the past decade's successes.

TRENDS IN ILLUSTRATION AND WRITING

Among the creators of children's picture books, Elizabeth Cleaver was a seminal figure. From her first publication in 1968 to her premature death in 1985, Cleaver's work encompasses many kinds of books—from the traditional illustrated book in which intermittent illustrations stand separate from the text (the poetry collections *The Wind Has Wings*, 1968 and *The New Wind Has Wings*, 1984) to the pure picture-book for the pre-school child (*ABC*, 1984). An original and innovative talent, Cleaver developed an unmistakable style with her striking sense of design, distinctive collage technique, and passion for blazing colour and rich texture.

Cleaver's fascination with the layered matter of mythology and archetypal imagery led her to illustrate legends of native peoples, a Magyar romance (*The Miraculous Hind*, 1973), and a Russian folktale-like ballet (*Petrouchka*, 1980). Her use of folk motifs from each culture, often repeated in hypnotic, stylized variations or friezes, add cultural authenticity and a ritualistic formality to her pictures. Like the illustrations of myths by the American illustrator Gerald McDermott, this use of details based on folk art places the story and pictures against a cultural backdrop and adds ceremonial dignity and weight to these ancient tales. And with her adroit sense of play Cleaver makes the pictures and story more comprehensible to children by using cut-out silhouettes, much like a child's toy paper dolls, and surprising configurations of collages, made from textured, coloured monoprints, torn and cut and integrated with linoprints. Her collage technique has a greater sensuality and evocativeness than the work of other internationally acclaimed picture-book collage artists, such as Ezra Jack Keats, Leo Lionni, and Eric Carle.

Cleaver introduces a spontaneous joy by including found art—real objects that startle and emerge from the page—such as a pearl, fur, lace, birch-bark, cedar, or an opening zipper. In *ABC* she unites her interest in typographical design and found art and moves away from the still, stylized grace and narrative flow of her early mythological pictures to a childlike rendering of the world's wonders. A compact book designed to fit comfortably into a child's hands, it opens like a solid, square treasure box to disclose the first mysteries of a child's world. This small book is very intense. The rainbow-brilliant colours of the alphabet letters and objects, and the physicality and weight of the shapes, which cast real shadows on the page, pack the book with mood and images lit up with a charged light like that before a storm.

The childlike quality of certain of Cleaver's cut-out figures is also found in the work of another pioneering illustrator—Ann Blades. Yet Cleaver's art is also the epitome of artifice—the creation of secondary realities, closed worlds of stylized folk images on the stage of myth or ballet. By contrast, Ann Blades's illustrations are absolutely natural and ingenuous, looking out to the physical world with a gentle love and warmth. She too is a kind of folk artist, having begun her career in the tradition of the self-taught illustrator. But Blades is not a truly naïve artist in the manner of such primitive picture-book illustrators as the American Mattie Lou O'Kelley. Blades's early works (*Mary of Mile 18*, 1971; *A Boy of Taché*, 1973; *A Salmon for Simon*, 1978; and *Pettranella*, 1980—the last two written by Betty Waterton) show the poignant delicacy of a childlike, naïve style in which draughtsmanship is tentative, the composition and shapes simplified, and the colour sense intuitive. And yet all elements combine to create an innocent, unsentimental simplicity of effect that underscores one of Blades's recurring themes—the vulnerability and certitude of childhood. One of the first Canadian illustrators to explore the theme of the multicultural experience as foreground and the power of a recognizable Canadian landscape as background, Blades focuses on specific children's lives. Her picture-books speak to the varieties and regionalism of Canadian life in the experiences of a British Columbia Mennonite girl, a West Coast Indian boy, a nineteenth-century European immigrant child in Manitoba.

Blades's illustrations, like Cleaver's, have been primarily narrative, but because they extend the longer text of the picture-storybook they are less fluid in relation to the story. The picture-storybook is differentiated from the classic picture-book by a less integrated relation between pictures and words. Blades's pictures are usually full-page illustrations, formally facing a page of text. In her one genuine picture-book, she focuses, like Cleaver, on the concept of the alphabet book: *By the Sea: An Alphabet Book* (1985). Here Blades's design sense is fully mature and confident. From the scalloped blue and white waves of the end papers to each of the framed pictures, the composition of letter and scene is clever and refined, showing a smoother draughtsmanship than her earlier work. The small paintings, set on a West Coast beach, balance the soft, sweeping lines of sand, ocean, and mountains with the smaller scale of children's seaside play. A narrative structure is provided by following a brother and sister from morning to sunset through their games and activities. Blades's watercolours are carefully controlled, and the clear, luminous colour washes have the delicate translucence of seaside light. The figures of the children recall her previous work in their paradoxically sturdy vulnerability and in the poetic rhythm of the visual images they inhabit, which are quiet and calm compositions even when the children are in full motion.

Ann Blades's *Mary of Mile 18* was the first full-colour picture-book published by Tundra Books. May Cutler, publisher of Tundra, has since commissioned respected gallery artists, such as William Kurelek, to interpret their childhood experiences in illustrations combined with non-fiction autobiographical texts that (unlike Ann Blades's insight into the immediacy of childhood) offer a set of nostalgic reminiscences of childhood as seen through adult eyes. The pictures that frame these memoirs are more like formal works of fine art than narrative illustrations. This group of artists has created picture-storybooks that often combine a consciously naïve or primitive art style with an interesting, but overlong or laboured text. Nonetheless, sophisticated works of art have been created by such Tundra author-illustrators as William Kurelek (*A Prairie Boy's Winter*, 1973, and other titles), John Lim (*At Grandmother's House*, 1977, and *Merchants of the Mysterious East*, 1981), Sing Lim (*West Coast Chinese Boy*, 1979), and Shizuye Takashima (*A Child in Prison Camp*, 1971).

Another group of Tundra artists has created uniquely regional alphabet books or works of dream-like, magic-realist pictures coupled with a fragmentary text, as in works by Ted Harrison (*A Northern Alphabet*, 1982 and *Children of the Yukon*, 1977), Warabé Aska (*Who Goes to the Park*, 1984), Allan Moak (*A Big City ABC*, 1984), and Stéphane Poulin (*Ah! belle cité!/A Beautiful City ABC*, 1985).

Many of these books follow the trend of European picture-book aesthetics, in which the illustrations are considered more important than the text, and the books become adult collectors' pieces rather than actual children's books. However, the illustrations in these works do succeed in creating a rich visual and imaginative experience. The books immerse the reader in a physical and cultural region. They give a strong sense and flavour of daily life at a particular time and in a particular place, which may be the exotic Singapore of the 1930s (as in John Lim's companion pieces *At Grandmother's House* and *Merchants of the Mysterious East*). But it is more likely to be an area and era closer to home—traversing the diverse regions and multicultural identities of Canada, from the thriving, contemporary urban centres of Quebec and Montreal in Miyuki Tanobe's *Québec Je t'aime/I Love You* (1976) and Stéphane Poulin's *Ah! belle cité!/A Beautiful City ABC* to Ukrainian-Canadian farm life in Depression-era Manitoba, as in William Kurelek's *A Prairie Boy's Winter* and *A Prairie Boy's Summer* (1975). These books also map the emotional and geographical topography of Canada; they travel across the country from east to west, from the Prince Edward Island of Lindee Climo's *Chester's Barn* (1982) to the Vancouver of Sing Lim's *West Coast Chinese Boy*. They range from north to south, from Ted Harrison's *Children of the Yukon* to the Toronto of Allan Moak's *A Big City ABC*.

The styles of the Tundra illustrators are as far-ranging as their choice of settings. The dream-like, Rousseauesque exoticism of John Lim's stylized paintings is perfectly appropriate for the cultural imagery of distant Singapore. His folk-art serigraphs are deliberately naïve, with a surface ornamental quality. They combine flat colours and decorative patterns with stylized forms that abandon outline and weight to float in asymmetrical compositions influenced by Oriental conventions of pictorial space. Human figures are columnar, resembling glazed pottery dolls, their identical faces on oddly angled heads. The magical quality of the visual imagery is well suited to a picaresque journey through a haunting tropical countryside and an alluring city rich in astrologers, story-tellers, and fortune-tellers.

Another legitimate pictorial travelogue is Miyuki Tanobe's warm love-letter to Montreal and Quebec—a bustling, joyous celebration of working-class life set against a panorama of restaurants, stores, lanes, back alleys, streets, and country spaces. With their comical doll-like figures that cluster around and hang out of toy-scale buildings, the overflowing pictures evoke the curving lines and Alice-in-Wonderland sense of scale of medieval paintings. The earthy tones and painterly style capture the textures of brick, stone, and snow in throbbing, rippling rhythms of a community bursting with life and gaiety.

Warabé Aska's *Who Goes to the Park* is another celebration—not of urban street life, but of a pastoral refuge at the heart of a large city—Toronto's High Park. Aska's illustrations are linked to a cycle of poems that form a paean to the park; they follow seasonal rhythms, from the springtime return of the Canada Geese to the mysterious winter ghost-shadows of the snow geese. Images of flight throughout the book emphasize the imaginative surrealism of the pictures. Aska's oil paintings have a magic-realist or surrealist dimension; his park seems an Escher-like double realm of the conscious and unconscious worlds. Naïvely styled figures drawn from the cultural mosaic of Canada fill the foreground in scenes of domestic genre painting as they indulge in relaxation, play, festivities. But these ordinary human park activities are bathed in an effulgent, eerily radiant light, and the sky itself is a playground of dream images. Angels, cherubim, wedding bells, and Buddhist thunder gods float in the sky like mysterious reflections—imaginative, psychological projections of the world below. This play with visual text and sub-text, with the transmutation of images, is similar to the effects created by the British illustrator Anthony Brown.

Another form of unearthly otherness appears in Ted Harrison's oil paintings of the Yukon. In *Children of the Yukon* and *A Northern Alphabet*, faceless, anonymous, generic figures—Indian, Inuit, and white—enact their daily round against a wild arctic background of psychedelic shapes and neon colours. The swirling, curvilinear style heavily outlines the flat shapes of figures and buildings like pieces of stained glass. Piercing, vertiginous streaks of unnaturally pure and manic colour represent the bleak landscape and endless sky, turning the north into an abstract state of mind as much as a realistic place.

The rich panoply of art styles and techniques of the Tundra series of *Canadian Children's Books as Works of Art* has definitely contributed to the maturing of children's-book illustration at home and has received international praise. Many of the Tundra productions, however, combine sophisticated, stunning art work with thin, weak, minimal, or adult-oriented texts. And, although the books are splendid works of art, they do not tell gripping stories. As vehicles for art, they resemble adult coffee-table books rather than real children's books designed with a child audience in mind; they are certainly more suitable for older school-aged children than for pre-school children.

Another group of picture-books published by Annick Press is more child-oriented in approach, philosophy, content, and style. This publisher concentrates on works for pre-schoolers and younger school-aged children. One of Annick's most popular illustrators is Michael Martchenko. His blithely insouciant watercolour and pencil illustrations are a light-hearted complement to texts by both Allen Morgan and Robert Munsch, which take a satirical, child-power stance, delighting in the oral story-telling and supreme silliness so loved by pre-schoolers. Martchenko's playful, spirited cartoon style has a spontaneous quality. With its loose, exuberant line and free application of colour, its witty detail and caricature, his illustrative art is a sturdier cousin to the droll, whimsical sketches by the British illustrator Quentin Blake.

And, like the exaggerated comic fantasies they illustrate, Martchenko's sketches could be set in any North American or Western European urban centre. The sense of place is an unspecified locale—home, neighbourhood yard and stoop, school and street—inside the domestic circle of the contemporary city or suburban child. The child figures are equally universal types. Competent kids drawn as down-to-earth, rumpled, and solid, they are active, self-reliant, spunky—the Jacob Two Twos of the picture-book set.

The pop-cartoon style of the illustrations perfectly reflects the nature of these tall-tale stories. The authors—Allen Morgan in his *Matthew* series (*Matthew and the Midnight Tow Truck*, 1984; *Matthew and the Midnight Turkeys*, 1985) and the prolific Robert Munsch (*The Paper Bag Princess*, 1980; *Mortimer*, 1985; *Thomas' Snowsuit*, 1985; *Murmel, Murmel, Murmel*, 1982; and others), whose numerous titles have been translated into several languages and are also available as recordings—write urban folktales. These tongue-in-cheek child satires show brave and plucky kids surviving absurd adventures, ingeniously extending the limits of their freedom, thwarting authority figures such as arrogant dragons, pompous mayors, curmudgeonly teachers and principals, and cold technology. The Munsch stories, especially, are comfortably colloquial, dramatically fast-paced, and texturally rich in sound patterns—oral ryhthm and onomatopoeia, refrains and repeated folk tags, and nonsense sounds that invite the child to participate.

Like the recited folktale, Munsch's cumulative or shaggy-dog stories were developed orally as he told them to groups of pre-schoolers.

Consequently they have a theatrical style and come alive when told and read aloud. This oral genesis pares away the non-essentials, resulting in a universal, internationally marketable contemporary folktale. These folklike 'every child' adventures are not particularly Canadian. (The dream-fantasy genre of Allen Morgan's *Matthew's Midnight Adventures* series has more in common with *In the Night Kitchen* (1963) by the American Maurice Sendak than with any Canadian cultural spirit.) But the casual and natural inclusion in Martchenko's illustrations for several of Munsch's texts of a racially and ethnically mixed group of children (with no comment in the text on this point) is true to Canada's multicultural society. The Martchenko pictures for the Munsch and Morgan publications are true to classic picture-book illustration in the sense that they extend the emotional tone of the stories and include visual gags in keeping with the slapstick humour of the texts. But many of the books themselves fall within the domain of the longer-text picture-storybook genre rather than within that of the true picture-book with its limited text and fully developed, interdependent relationship between pictures and words.

Three aesthetically successful Canadian picture-books in which illustrations and text do form an indivisible whole are Ian Wallace's *Chin Chiang and the Dragon's Dance* (1984, illustrated by the author), Tim Wynne-Jones's *Zoom at Sea* (1983, illustrated by Ken Nutt), and Maryann Kovalski's *Brenda and Edward* (1984, illustrated by the author). Wallace's surreal, iridescent pen-and-ink and watercolour pictures, Ken Nutt's sculptural black and white graphite drawings, and Kovalski's gentle, sketchy cartoons in gouache, coloured pencil, and pen and ink are worlds apart in style and technique. But these illustrators all succeed in extending and illuminating their stories in film-like sequencing, in creating visual counterpoints to the text, in amplifying detail, and in elucidating the theme through visual images. And in all three books the texts speak with a strong, personal voice; they are composed of very few words, selected for precision of meaning, freshness of diction, and fluid musicality.

From his early picture-book *The Sandwich* (1975, created with Angela Wood)—one of the first contemporary Canadian picture-book treatments of the subject of urban, ethnically mixed children—to his Inuit adventure, *Very Last First Time* (1985), written by Jan Andrews, Ian Wallace has consistently explored the multicultural

Canadian mosaic. For *Chin Chiang and the Dragon's Dance* Wallace immersed himself in the Chinese-Canadian community. He researched traditions and customs for this story of a young Chinese-Canadian boy who comes to terms with his culture by overcoming his fears and resolving to join his grandfather in the dragon dance of the Chinese New Year celebration. There are intriguing parallels between this work and Maurice Sendak's *Where the Wild Things Are*, both in content and in the way the illustrations extend the text to explore a child's emotional crisis and growth into maturity. From Chin Chiang's flight from his responsibilities to his final, triumphant procession in the dance, the book's sub-text is that life is motion, dance, change. Like Sendak, Wallace expresses the metaphorical sub-text in illustrations that are fittingly choreographic. Fluid with motion, they ripple in spiralling compositions like a dragon's tail, echoing the first magnificent glimpse of the dragon dance on the cover. The simple, straightforward text allows space for the pictures to add emotional resonance. As the dramatic conflict in the story builds, the illustrations change dynamically in perspective and size (reflecting the boy's emotional growth) and in tonal intensity until the traditional, bright Chinese red dominates, signifying resolution and joy. Vistas of sky and flight—images of flying pigeons and sweeping dragon costumes—carry the theme that Chin Chiang will learn to dance, to fly in a spiritual sense. Like Max of *Where the Wild Things Are*, whose crowned portrait appears on the dragon-spiralled library staircase, Chin Chiang will, in his own way, also return from his adventures a king. The concrete story is given a mythic overtone through the visual motifs and dreamlike, delicate surrealism of the paintings. Even the setting is dreamlike. Despite the recognizable vistas of Vancouver's street signs, buildings, mountains, and sea, and of architectural details from Victoria, this Chinatown goes unnamed; it is meant to stand for every Chinatown in North America. The haunting colours—sometimes as flashingly iridescent as dragon scales, sometimes luminous with the soft, lambent West-Coast light—help to propel the story into a mythic dimension.

Whereas the dream-like surrealism in the illustrations for *Chin Chiang and the Dragon's Dance* tends to heighten the realism of the story by contrasting it with an inner mythic resonance, *Zoom at Sea* works in the opposite direction. A quest fantasy, it is grounded in reality by the restrained firmness of Ken Nutt's down-to-earth, matter-of-fact pencil drawings. Although Tim Wynne-Jones's evocative, musically rhythmic text is as spare and smooth as a folk-tale, and Maria, the gypsy keeper of the mysterious Victorian house, is as mythic as the enigmatic goddess-characters in George MacDonald's fantasies, the whimsical concept of a cat's quest for the sea and the miracle of an expanding ocean vista inside a hidden room require concrete illustrations to make the story believable and anchor the fantasy in reality. Both the ordinary and the supernatural images are rendered with meticulous detail. Ken Nutt's art work recalls the detailed draughtsmanship, fine rendering, black and white tonal variations, and monumental weight of the graphite pictures of the American illustrator Chris Van Allsburg. But Ken Nutt's wit in the sly details that anthropomorphize Zoom—the curious, eternally searching cat—is gentler than that of Allsburg.

The concept of an infinite house with rooms that expand into an endless space of imaginative freedom and exploration has yielded a sequel, *Zoom Away* (1985), in which the humour is even more subtle: Zoom appears as the perfect bourgeois—contentedly knitting in his oversized armchair with *People* magazine slyly by his side.

The same gentle humour pervades Maryann Kovalski's *Brenda and Edward*. Kovalski tells a tender fable of animal friendship in the tradition of the Americans Arnold Lobel (*Frog and Toad Are Friends*, 1970) and James Marshall (*George and Martha*, 1972) and the Canadian Patti Stren, whose tongue-in-cheek narratives (*Hug Me*, 1977; *Sloan and Philamina*, 1979) are integrated with comic-strip dialogue balloons, minimal, witty line drawings, and absurdist sight gags. Kovalski's humour is more subtle, an element of a delicate sensibility. In a fine collaboration of art and text, Kovalski's anthropomorphized dog protagonists love and lose each other, only to be reunited in their old age. The unfinished sketchiness and pastel tones add to the tale's delicate blend of sentiment and understated humour. This simple story, told in a smooth, fluid style, is extended emotionally by the affectionate cartoons, which are full of expressive characterization and poignant details that reveal the couple's deep love and contentment. Interesting shifts from aerial perspectives to dog's-eye views signify the powerlessness of an animal in a human world.

Even an overview that merely skims the last decade's achievements in picture-books must acknowledge the tremendous diversity of artistic styles and the proliferation of media generated by the illustrators. Examples of recently published picture-books with fresh, new illustrative styles are legion, and what follows is a mere sample. Phoebe Gilman employs ink and gouache freely in an illuminated manuscript style that highlights the anachronistic wit in her comic literary fairy-tale *The Balloon Tree* (1984). Scot Ritchie's cartoons add a satirical *New Yorker*-style bite to *Dinner at Auntie Rose's* (1984). Karen Patkau's collage art in *Don't Eat Spiders* (1985) combines child-like exuberance with a three-dimensional depiction of imaginative play. Barbara Reid's tenderly sculpted and textured plasticine models and unusual perspectives charmingly depict farm life in *The New Baby Calf* (1984). Lindee Climo's dramatic sense of design and the curvilinear contour-lines in her paintings for *Chester's Barn* (1982) recall folk carving. Marie-Louise Gay's expressionistic ink-and-watercolour cartoons for *Lizzy's Lion* (1984) combine caricature and grotesquerie, echoing sophisticated cartoonists such as Ralph Steadman, Tomi Ungerer, and that great absurdist Edward Lear. Michèle Lemieux's evocative watercolours for *What Is That Noise?* (1984) have a European sensibility.

TRENDS IN FORMAT AND THEME

Besides offering an impressive range of illustrative styles and techniques, as exemplified by the Canadian picture-books under discussion here, contemporary picture-books also show diversity in type and format. There now exist more *kinds* of picture-books than ever before, designed for children's different developmental stages, interests, and needs, and created with a variety of purposes and intents. It is only in the last few years that Canadian picture-books have acquired this diversity, as publishers have adapted international trends to the Canadian market. These include, among others, wordless picture-books, concept books, alphabet and counting books, toy books, and single illustrated poems, songs, and folktales.

Toy Books

The unusual format or toy book, with paper-engineering feats and graphic gimmicks—pop-ups, push-and-pull tabs, movable parts, and split or die-cut pages—has a large international following. Interestingly,

Canadian publishers have not jumped onto this peripheral 'semi-book' bandwagon. Except for the book, game, and puzzle combination in Roger Paré's boxed activity set, *The Annick ABC Activity Set* (1985), the few other productions are designed and executed by non-Canadians or acquired through the purchase of foreign rights or joint publication, as were *The Yellow House* (1982), a flap-page book by Grete Janus Hertz and Iben Clante, Frank Asch's cut-out *I Can Blink* (1985) and *I Can Roar* (1985), and Matthew Price's and Jean Claverie's pop-up *Peekaboo!* (1985). Instead, publishers such as Annick, Tundra, and James Lorimer have issued series of mini-books, in the tradition of Beatrix Potter's 'little books for little hands'. In a clever marketing strategy, Annick publishes the 'Annikins', small 3½-inch-square paperbacks (often miniature reprints of larger format originals such as the Munsch titles) designed for mass-market distribution and selling for 99¢.

The miniature *Jumblebooks* series published by James Lorimer are witty, wordless puzzles illustrated by Philippe Béha. And the paperback Tundra series, *Mini Books for Mini Hands*, combines minimal line art with gracefully simple stories in a bilingual text.

Books for Babies and Toddlers

Another extremely popular, ubiquitous international trend is the board-book for babies, usually designed for children under two or three. James Lorimer and Tundra have produced several ingenious and aesthetically pleasing series in this area—some wordless and some with a minimal text. Tundra's wordless *The Baabee Books* series, designed by Dayal Kaur Khalsa, is a stepped, three-part series focusing on identification and recognition skills for children from infancy (with foldout friezes such as *Baabee 1: Here's Baabee*, 1983) to the age of three (with laminated board-books such as *Happy Birthday, Baabee*, 1984). Stylized figures of babies and simple domestic objects are rendered in flat blocks of brilliant colour heavily outlined in black. These extremely clear and graphically compelling symbols give the books a futuristic, space-age look, including the appealing but curiously unisex, uni-race babies (one of whom is neon-blue).

James Lorimer publishes three series of board books. Illustrated in full colour with Gallic vivacity and charm by Philippe Béha (among others), they were originally published in French by the Quebec publisher, Éditions Ovale. Experimental in format, the *Jumblebooks* (such as Béha's *Getting Dressed*, 1985) are tiny three-inch-square wordless creations. The *Little Big Books* (in such titles as Marie-Louise Gay's *The Garden*, 1985) contain foldout, accordion-style pictures on such themes as train, tree, house, and street. Cinematic in concept, one side is a wordless frieze of lively, detailed images portraying a scene or vignette. On the other side is a list of vocabulary and identifying close-ups. The intent is educational, but these are more than teaching tools. The *Tot-Books* series, for example, includes simple stories or vignettes written by Sylvie Assathiany and Louise Pelletier, which are designed as child-rearing aids; the stories explore such themes as sibling rivalry or toilet training, all in twelve to sixteen lines. Although the truncated texts have none of the hypnotic music or rhythms of nursery rhymes or full picture-books, the tone is not didactic, especially in the titles concerning Little Bear and his family (such as *Grandma's Visit*, 1985), in which domestic warmth and identification with the protagonists are as strong as they are in the American Rosemary Wells's board-books about small animals.

This international publishing trend towards picture-books for infants and toddlers is a response to an increasing awareness on the part of educators, librarians, and parents that children can enjoy the language and pictures of picture-books at a much younger age than previously supposed. Beyond the board-books, some picture-books focus with simplicity, clarity, and warm humour on the minutiae of everyday experiences and small, domestic dramas of young pre-schoolers. There has also been a flood of child-rearing adjuncts that have little imaginative integrity or emotional impact: works that explore both the problem-solving and developmental tasks of pre-schoolers and the concerns of parents. Such books make bland bibliotherapy and dry educational tools.

There are certain titles and series, however, that rise above this tide of mediocrity and didacticism. The *Annick Toddler Series* contains numerous works that epitomize the best of the genre. Kathy Stinson's *Red is Best* (1982) and *Big or Little?* (1983)—both illustrated by Robin Baird Lewis—create the same atmosphere of unfolding delight in the world and emotional reassurance that mark the domestic classics for this age group by the British author-illustrators John Burningham,

By MARYANN KOVALSKI for *Brenda and Edward* (Kids Can Press, 1984)

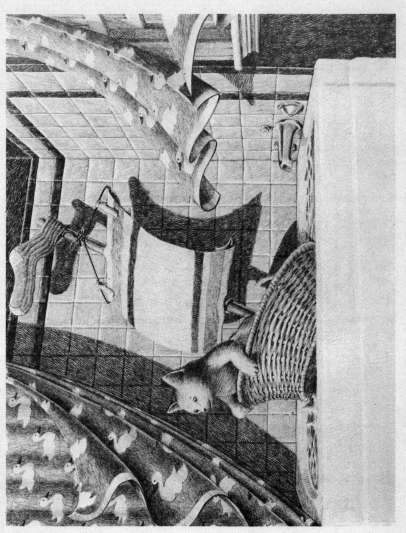

By KEN NUTT for Tim Wynne-Jones's *Zoom at Sea* (Groundwood Books, 1983)

34

By ANN BLADES for *By the Sea, An Alphabet Book* (Kids Can Press, 1985)

By ELIZABETH CLEAVER for *The Enchanted Caribou* (Oxford, 1985)

Helen Oxenbury, and Shirley Hughes. In *Red is Best*, the story of a little girl's obsessive love for the colour red and her defence of the colour against her mother's pragmatic suggestions is told in the first person as a miniature, intimate character study. The text and illustrations are in perfect balance. The repetitive, rhythmic text flows with an unpretentious, natural grace. Pen-and-ink line drawings capture the child's spontaneous energy, while splashes of red and bright red endpapers provide graphic unity and transmit the child's emotional attachment to the colour.

Other toddler titles that show similar originality of treatment are Gail Chislett's *The Rude Visitors* (1984, illustrated by Barbara Di Lella), Andrea Wayne von Königslöw's *Toilet Tales* (1985), and Emily Hearn's *Woosh! I Hear a Sound* (1983, illustrated by Heather Collins).

Social Realism

Parent-child relationships, sex roles, and social attitudes and values are common themes of modified social realism in many of the picture-books published by such social-activist, alternative presses as Annick Press, Women's Press, and Kids Can Press. The focus may range widely across the social spectrum—from parental separation and divorce, as in Kathy Stinson's *Mom and Dad Don't Live Together Any More* (1984, illustrated by Nancy Lou Reynolds), to the disabled child, as in Emily Hearn's *Good Morning Franny, Good Night Franny* (1984, illustrated by Mark Thurman). But in the plethora of titles addressing such issues, very few are memorable as stories or illustrative art. They are more often disposable bibliotherapy, created to fill a perceived educational need.

An original note is struck, however, by Priscilla Galloway's *When You Were Little and I Was Big* (1984, illustrated by Heather Collins) in its presentation of a clever mother-daughter role reversal. The daughter's thoughts on caring for her mother are visualized in the illustrations, which depict a reversal in both the nurturing relationship and the size of the mother and daughter.

One of the first books in this area is also a real classic: Sue Ann Alderson's *Bonnie McSmithers, You're Driving Me Dithers* (1974, illustrated by Fiona Garrick). The humorous, psychologically honest relationship between an independent, mischievous child and her long-suffering artist-mother is punctuated by strong prose rhythms and rhyming refrains; the music of language is the key to the success of the *Bonnie* series.

Concept Books

Another picture-book sub-genre—concept books—encompasses a broad spectrum of ideas and formats, including the traditional alphabet and counting book. An unusual Canadian concept book is Joan Bodger's *Belinda's Ball* (1981, illustrated by Mark Thurman), which is based on Jean Piaget's psychological theories of object constancy and representation. Language development is encouraged by printing some of the text in red to involve children in the story.

Language development through the recognition of letters, words, vocabulary, and speech patterns is also one major purpose of the alphabet book. Both Elizabeth Cleaver's *ABC* and Ann Blades's *By the Sea: An Alphabet Book* create an enriched language experience through traditional letter symbols, basic vocabulary, and visual representation, with isolated images in the former and a continuous narrative and single setting for context and continuity in the latter. The group of alphabet books from Tundra discussed previously celebrate a specific region or city: Ted Harrison, the Yukon; Allan Moak, Toronto; Stéphane Poulin, Montreal.

Bilingual and multilingual alphabet and counting books also reflect Canada's multicultural heritage. Both Barbara Wilson's bilingual *ABC et/and 123* (1980, illustrated by Gisèle Daigle) and Poulin's *Ah! belle cité!/A Beautiful City ABC* contain words chosen for oral, visual, and aural similarities between the two languages. Angela Wood's *Kids Can Count* (1976) combines black and white photographs in the urban style of the American Tana Hoban with a counting text in English, French, Chinese, Italian, and Greek.

Children's own art has graced Canadian alphabet and counting books in such earlier works as Anne and Alex Wyse's *Alphabet Book* (1968) and *The One to Fifty Book* (1973), both of which contain the art work of native Indian children. Native children's art is once again found in the vital *Byron and His Balloon: An English-Chipewyan Counting Book* (1984). David May's bilingual counting text in English and Chipewyan-Indian characters was created to link the series of

children's ingenuous watercolour paintings of life in the Saskatche-
wan Indian community of La Loche.

Bilingual Books and Translations

Bilingual and multilingual picture-books whose texts exceed the
restrictions of the alphabet book or counting book have grown in
number and quality in the past decade as bilingual education programs
have increased throughout Canada. Many are published as bilingual
English/French editions, with the text in both languages rendered on
the same page, or on facing pages. Tundra is particularly conscientious
in this regard, issuing picture-storybooks with lavish illustrations and
extended texts in both languages, such as Miyuki Tanobe's *Québec
Je t'aime/I Love You*, Felix Vincent's *Catlands/Pays des chats* (1977),
and Jacques de Roussan's *Beyond the Sun/Au-dèla du soleil* (1977),
and *If I Came from Mars/Si j'étais martien* (1977). Tundra also
publishes *Mini Books for Mini Hands*, an inexpensive series of animal
tales written in a playful, spare style in both languages and illustrated
in minimal line art. This quartet of books, which contains such titles
as Philip Stratford's *Olive A Dog/Un chien* (1976), is designed for a
very young audience.

Kids Can Press is another publisher committed to bilingual picture-
books, ranging from their *Folktale Series* of single illustrated tales in
English and the language of origin to the straightforward, informational
French-English productions by Marion Schaffer and Kathy Vanderlinden, such as *I Love My Cat!/J'aime mon chat!* (1980). Lesley
Fairfield's three bilingual word books for beginning readers, such as
Let's Go/Allons-y! (1983), are without a story structure, but the series
contains an enticing, riotous display of pictures and an identifying
bilingual vocabulary followed by language puzzles and games.

The most original approach to the concept of a bilingual picture-
book is the single-text integration of French and English in Madeline
Kronby's *A Secret in My Pocket* (1977, illustrated by Anna Vojtech).
The natural, colloquial ease of the bilingual narrative and dialogue
owes much to the author's experience as a script writer for the CBC's
bilingual children's program 'Chez Hélène'.

Apart from bilingual editions, translations into English from French-
language picture-books originally published in Quebec have increased in

the last decade. (In earlier years such books were almost totally non-existent.) Picture-books by author-illustrators, such as Roger Paré (*A Friend Like You*, 1984), and picture-storybooks by well-known writers for adults, such as Gabrielle Roy (*Cliptail*, 1980, illustrated by François Olivier) and Roch Carrier (*The Hockey Sweater*, 1984, illustrated by Sheldon Cohen), have gained a new audience in English Canada. But perhaps the most popular has been Ginette Anfousse. Anfousse's *My Friend Pichou* series explores the changeable, day-to-day emotions and adventures of an irrepressible little girl and her toy aardvark. The simple, first-person text, confiding and whimsical, and the stylized poster-bright pictures possess a piquant humour as well as a Tomi Ungerer–like anarchic vitality.

Not surprisingly, a young child's relationship with a snowman has been a theme treated in both French- and English-language picture-books, from the bright, comic snapshot images of Cécile Gagnon's *Snowfeather* (1980, originally published in French) to Allen Morgan's poignant *Sadie and the Snowman* (1985, illustrated by Brenda Clark). As quintessentially Canadian as this subject may seem, such successes as the British illustrator Raymond Brigg's *The Snowman* (1978) remind us that the concept is universal.

Beginning Readers

In whatever language they are written, beginning readers, or read-aloud books for children on the threshold of learning to read, pose particular difficulties of creation. Compared to the rich, musical language of the traditional picture-book, which is intended to be read aloud by an adult to a child, the beginning-reader books must cope with the severe restrictions of short, simple sentences and a basic, controlled vocabulary. Few writers succeed in working within these tight confines to create works as memorable or sophisticated as the *Frog and Toad* series by the American Arnold Lobel. In Canada, they are rare indeed.

Allen Morgan's attempts in the *Kids-Can-Read* series include two chapter-structured readers—*Christopher and the Elevator Closet* (1981, illustrated by Franklin Hammond) and *Molly and Mr Maloney* (1982, illustrated by Maryann Kovalski)—and one reader with a picture-book format, *Christopher and the Dream Dragon* (1984, illustrated by Brenda Clark). The texts are serviceable for their purpose, and have, at times, a certain fantastical charm. On the whole, however, the restrictions of the genre curtail the off-beat, exaggerated silliness and dream-like logic that are so attractive in Morgan's longer *Matthew* picture-books.

The publisher James Lorimer has placed much emphasis on social issues and problems of Canadian identities in the *Kids of Canada* beginning-reader series. Very few of the titles have any literary merit or story appeal, despite the recruitment of well-known writers for adults, but there is some interest in the cumulative, folktale-like structure of *Anna's Pet* (1980) by Margaret Atwood and Joyce Barkhouse and in the suspenseful plot of lost animals in a dark wood in *Six Darn Cows* (1979) by Margaret Laurence. Both of these books benefit from Ann Blades's attractive art work. In this series, however, the only title that succeeds in reaching beyond the reader-genre boundaries is Selwyn Dewdney's historical *The Hungry Time* (1980), illustrated by Olena Kassian. There is intrinsic drama in the Mississauga Indian family's struggle against starvation and the escape of a brother and sister from a bear.

Also historical in setting, and still primarily a reader (albeit with a longer text), is Meguido Zola's *Moving* (1983), illustrated by Victoria Cooper. Interestingly, this story of a Hutterite child living on the Canadian Prairies in the 1930s was published outside Canada by the British publisher Julia MacRae Books in the *Blackbird* extended-reader series. The simple evocative text conveys a deep feeling for the stern and loving Hutterite community and builds a series of authentically childlike perceptions of change. Little Becky's fear of moving and leaving behind what she loves is one of the principal themes of Canadian children's literature—that of being a stranger, of moving to a new place, or immigrating to a new land. This subject occurs frequently in the traditional picture-book and the longer picture-storybook and is one facet of the larger multicultural experience so central to Canadian children's literature.

Themes of Immigration, Multiculturalism, and Regionalism

Picture-books and picture-storybooks that look at the experience of immigration may be examples of contemporary realism or historical fiction. It is interesting that the historical titles are more emotionally effective and cleverly conceived than those that focus on contemporary social realities. The picture-books presenting new Canadian children adjusting to contemporary multicultural urban life, although well-meaning, have a strong didactic bent, an overly earnest tone, and scant literary skill. But despite their literary flaws, such works as Yvonne Singer's *Little-Miss-Yes-Miss* (1976, illustrated by Angela Wood), Carol Pasternak's and Allen Sutterfield's *Stone Soup* (1974, illustrated by Hedy Campbell), and Ian Wallace and Angela Wood's *The Sandwich*, do have a forthright, unpretentious authenticity.

But for narrative appeal and quality of illustration, the works set in an earlier era of Canadian history and in regions other than metropolitan Toronto are much stronger. In two picture-storybooks—Betty Waterton's *Pettranella* (illustrated by Ann Blades) and Shelley Tanaka's *Michi's New Year* (1980, illustrated by Ron Berg)—the authors create an emotional realism that goes beyond their surface social realism. Both are stories of a young girl's adjustment to a new and alien country. The experiences of losing cultural value and identity, of rediscovering a sense of self, and of belonging in a new Canadian context are conveyed through both art and text.

In *Pettranella* a girl and her parents come from an unspecified country in nineteenth-century Europe to homestead in Manitoba. A love-gift from the girl's grandmother—seeds to be planted and to bloom as flowers in the new land, linking Pettranella to her past life in memory and beauty—is to provide the continuity between her two lives in two different countries. Her loss of the seeds and rediscovery of them in the form of glowing flowers in the spring symbolize the painful separation from her past life and acceptance of the new. The quiet tone of the clear, fluid writing is amplified by Ann Blades's watercolour paintings, whose subtle modulations of colour convey the emotional transition from old country to new and from harsh winter to soft spring. Dark, cramped images in sombre tones of European city streets and immigration depots are contrasted with lambent images of journeys across opening spaces as vast horizons unfold under fresh skies.

Michi's New Year, a title in PMA Books' *Northern Lights* series, admirably attempts to provide Canadian historical fiction for younger school-age children. Six small, square-shaped, picture-storybooks present different cultural groups in the context of particular periods in Canadian history. Historical fiction in picture-book or picture-storybook format, however, is notoriously difficult to write. The most effective seem to be those that eschew a wealth of historical detail and focus instead on the particular and the miniature: on individual, strongly characterized children responding to daily incidents in their lives. Historical detail may be extended through the illustrations, a formula used by the American Brinton Turkle in his stories of a young Quaker boy, which are so much more appealing than the fine but static historical picture-books of the British writer Fiona French.

Of the *Northern Lights* series, *Michi's New Year* is the most successful because of its integrity of emotion, in-depth characterization, and the restraint and dignity with which it tells the young girl's story. Other titles in the series—such as *The Last Ship* (1980), *Streets of Gold* (1980), *The Sky Caribou* (1980), *The Buffalo Hunt* (1980), and *The Yellow Flag* (1980)—are far-ranging in historical setting, dramatic in incident, and handsomely produced. They succeed in introducing young children to the colour and texture of Canadian history, but many of them attempt too much in broad historical scope and forfeit the slice-of-life, emotional reality that makes *Michi's New Year* a compelling story. Shelley Tanaka's writing style—natural, low-keyed, and childlike in the portrayal of a young immigrant Japanese girl's perceptions of Canadian life in the Vancouver of 1912—is especially graceful. Michi is homesick and alienated. Her emotional state is echoed (as in *Pettranella*) in Ron Berg's meticulous illustrations. The images of Japan are colourful and vivacious, full of social life and busy activity, contrasting poignantly with the lonely emptiness of the dull, wintry-brown Vancouver streets leached of colour and emotion. Through his use of Japanese folk-art motifs and designs in the decorative borders, and in pictures that recall Hokusai's wave and other Japanese wood-block prints, Berg's delicate illustrations convey the need to keep cultural customs and traditions alive. Colour and new life suffuse the illustrations and Michi's spirit as she comes into contact with a Westerner—a Vancouver boy—whose New Year's greeting parallels the warm ritual of the traditional Japanese New Year's celebration.

Tundra's series of autobiographical memoirs in picture-storybook format also considers in a historical context what it is like to grow up in the Canadian mosaic, what a Canadian identity means for a child in relation to diverse cultural heritages. In Sing Lim's *West Coast Chinese Boy*, William Kurelek's *A Prairie Boy's Winter* (and other titles), and Shizuye Takashima's *A Child in Prison Camp*, the memories of childhood and of the conflict between Canadian culture and the original ethnic culture of the parents is often tempered by the universality of art, for the child in each book grows up to be an artist. As Sing Lim says in *West Coast Chinese Boy*: 'The struggle between being Chinese and being Canadian, between Chinese culture that was so important to my parents' generation, and Canadian culture, I resolved in my own way. I found in art a more universal culture . . .'

As well as portraying the conventional childhood experiences of daily family life and social festivities and the exploration and discovery of the outside world, these works convey fear, anger, and bewilderment as hardship and prejudice are remembered. They range from the daily intolerance of, and latent violence against, the Chinese in Vancouver's Chinatown of the early 1920s (*West Coast Chinese Boy*) to the internment of the Japanese in the Second World War (*A Child in Prison Camp*).

Sing Lim's work brims with frenzied activity in the episodic text and plentiful illustrations. Sophisticated monotype glass paintings, numerous pen-and-ink sketches, and dancing, childlike scrawls overflow the margins. Sing Lim's recounting of his childhood experiences— from visits to traditional Chinese herbalists and the opera, to bear-paw feasts—is quite different in its lively, laughing tone from the simple gravity of Takashima's unresentful record of internment in the mountainous Kootenay region of British Columbia. With too weighty a text to be an actual picture-storybook, *A Child in Prison Camp* resembles a cinematic autobiography in its series of fragmentary daily vignettes. The muted watercolour paintings in an impressionistic style—haunting landscapes and blurred figures—are washed in a haze of emotion and memory.

Like Takashima's work, William Kurelek's memories of a Ukrainian-Canadian childhood spent on a Manitoba dairy farm in the 1930s form a set of seasonal interludes rendered in striking paintings that are loosely linked by a straightforward, somewhat dry text. *A Prairie Boy's Winter*, *A Prairie Boy's Summer*, and *Lumberjack* (1974) chronicle the boy William's growth into adulthood, and, in a sense, function as a sequential character study rather than as a plotted narrative. One of the constants in texts that describe changing seasonal activities—farm chores and children's games—is the solid characterization of William as a clumsy, unathletic loser in sports and games, a dreamer and artist with little social success; William is an outsider, a watcher. Another constant is the artwork from book to book; the adult artist depicts his child self engaged in close, intense observation of human behaviour and of animal life dwarfed by the endless prairie. The glowing nostalgia of the naïve style of the illustrations—solid, Breughelian child figures neatly frozen in formal compositions against the vast horizon—is in curious contrast to the text's psychological tone of troubled childhood with its sad refrain of the outcast's experience. Overpowering all other elements in the art and text is the sense of place—from the farms of Manitoba to the lumber camps of Northern Ontario and Quebec—of human life in relation to the land and climate.

In *A Northern Nativity* (1976) Kurelek moves from memoir to dream and legend. He sets one of the most resonant of narratives, the nativity, against a kaleidoscope of Canadian scenes. Based on a series of childhood dreams, the paintings place the nativity in the time of Kurelek's own childhood memories and relocate it in a cinematic journey across Canada. The holy family, depicted as representing all Canadians from the foothills of the Rocky Mountains to Ottawa, appears in many changing cultural identities, including Inuit, black, and Indian.

The landscape is a challenge and a character in its own right in another autobiographical picture-storybook, *Peter Pitseolak's Escape from Death* (1977). In this memoir the Arctic tundra is not an abstraction or a backdrop, but a concrete presence and mortal danger to Pitseolak, an Inuit artist of Baffin Island. Pitseolak's account of his escape with his stepson from a floating ice-field has the tone of heroic legend, not only in the plain, courageous narrative, but also in the artist's moving faith in the spirit world and in his stoic resolution. The sixteen mixed-media drawings in coloured felt pen, crayon, and pencil ingenuously portray small, ordinary people against a stark landscape populated by wild animals and visionary, dreamlike spirits.

The striking, elemental reality of the north and its harsh, unearthly beauty also inform the imagery of Jan Andrews's *Very Last First Time*, illustrated by Ian Wallace. In this picture-storybook, a contemporary Inuit girl walks alone, gathering mussels on the bottom of the sea while the tide is out. The realistic detail of her preparations for her descent under the ice and the exact descriptions of the seabed make this extraordinary experience completely credible, while the surrealistic paintings laden with half-hidden images emphasize the eerie, dreamlike dimension of the descent into the underworld. Although the marvellous premise of a child's adventure on the bottom of the sea and the threat of the returning tide, do not fulfil their dramatic potential, the child's interaction with the landscape is compelling.

The same bond between child and environment is portrayed in Betty Waterton's *A Salmon for Simon* (illustrated by Ann Blades), in which a West Coast Indian boy's desire for a salmon is the basis for a story redolent of the rain forest. Ann Blades's earth-toned watercolour washes capture the misty skies, wet sweep of sea, shoreline, and straggling village houses.

Small, independent presses such as Pemmican Publications work diligently to provide picture-books delineating native Indian and Métis life. Bernelda Wheeler (*I Can't Have Bannock, but the Beaver Has a Dam*, 1984) and Peter Eyvindson (*Kyle's Bath*, 1984) have written realistic but flawed stories of contemporary native children. More successful is Meguido Zola and Angela Dereume's *Nobody* (1983, illustrated by Wendy Wolsak), which adds an extra dimension of humour and psychological realism to the family story through the children's invention of a michievous 'Nobody', an imaginative child-surrogate reminiscent of trickster figures, such as Raven from native folklore.

Single Illustrated Folk-tales and Legends

The single illustrated folk-tale or legend is another area of Canadian picture-book publishing that has increased in variety and quality in the last decade. Throughout international children's-book publishing the phenomenal proliferation of single editions of folk-tales has meant a deluge of illustrators interpreting the same text in a wide range of styles and media. The value of this trend is questionable when illustration becomes a vehicle for the work of artists rather than an illumination of meaning. Nonetheless, it is possible for different illustrators to re-animate old tales by creating fresh versions.

In Canada, two illustrators (Laszlo Gal and Robin Muller) have reinterpreted classic European folk-tales. Laszlo Gal's art in an Italian High Renaissance style is grave and romantic with its poised, sculptural figures and delicate, pastel tones. He has illustrated Janet Lunn's retelling of *The Twelve Dancing Princesses* (1979) and Margaret Maloney's version of Hans Christian Andersen's *The Little Mermaid* (1983). In both works the texts are full and sensual—perfect read-aloud stories of dramatic suspense and romance, with richly cadenced, colourful language.

Gal's gouache and watercolour paintings do not extend these stories in the manner of pure picture-book illustrations. His art belongs to the tradition of lavish book illustration; the theatrical pictures heighten the drama and poignancy of these serious, even sombre, stories with visual vignettes, often formally framed, that stand separate from the text, offering windows into the world of faerie. The figures are of monumental solidity; they seem posed forever in frozen, graceful movements. They are affecting in their ordinariness—durable peasantry in the garb of prince and princess.

By contrast, Robin Muller's princes and princesses, in his pencil-crayon and ink illustrations for *Mollie Whuppie and the Giant* (1982), *Tatterhood* (1984), and *The Sorcerer's Apprentice* (1985), suffer from the slick prettiness and characterlessness that afflict the folklore illustrations of the American Susan Jeffers. Muller's fine draughtsmanship and irregular compositions convey a heightened drama and a potent atmosphere, and his style has elements of bold wit—especially evident in the satirical illustrations for *Tatterhood*—but the restrictions of a style reminiscent of commercial art keep Muller's versions from attaining Gal's memorable imagery.

The art of both Gal and Muller has a quality of suspended motion: Gal's scenes seem to be frozen in a dream, while Muller's resemble stylized cinematic stills. Two other picture-books based on legends drawn from ballet also attempt to link the movement of dance to mood and atmosphere: *Petrouchka*, retold and illustrated by Elizabeth Cleaver, and *The Nutcracker* (1985), retold by Veronica Tennant and illustrated by Toller Cranston.

The story by Igor Stravinsky and Alexandre Benois of the clown-puppet Petrouchka—his love for a ballerina-puppet and his death and spiritual rebirth—is illustrated by Cleaver with appropriate lino cuts built up of separate, movable body parts that capture the spirit of the articulated puppets. They appear to move with the stilted awkwardness of toy dolls, animated by a spirit of dance into a fluid grace. Each image is formally framed above the separately framed text; this device replicates the spectator's experience of viewing a ballet or puppetshow through the proscenium arch of a stage.

Scenes of Petrouchka's sad, lovelorn ballet and of the ballerina's flirtatious dance for the Moor are presented in a series of vertical panels that use the continuous-narrative technique. This device accentuates the awkward grace of the puppets' dances; the steps are isolated and jerky but, like the frames of an animated film, they become fluid when viewed as a unity. The radiant colours of the cut-and-pasted monoprint collages and the Russian folk-art patterns in traditional costume and design add a lavish, winter carnival atmosphere to the tragic story.

The graphic restraint and sequential story-telling of Cleaver's art in *Petrouchka* are in direct contrast to the overwhelming flood of Toller Cranston's art in *The Nutcracker*. Tennant's lengthy text returns to the original E.T.A. Hoffmann tale with its dark ambiguities and psychological tensions. Cranston's full-colour, phantasmagorical paintings and black and white vignettes embrace the hectic drama and baroque splendour of the story, but distract from, rather than add to, a unified piece of book design. The sinuous, psychedelic line and overripe colours bring a decorative exoticism to the story. Eclectic allusions to the classic book illustration by Kay Nielson and Edmund Dulac and to Middle-Eastern and Asiatic art styles evoke a dream magic. The story's dream power is foreshadowed in the frontispiece of the magus-like Grandfather Drosselmeyer smoking an opium pipe, emitting smoke phantasms from the ballet. Nevertheless—unlike Maurice Sendak's version of the Nutcracker, which remains true to the psychological themes and responds to the concept of ballet set design in book format—the work's final effect is that of a cluttered and vertiginous collection of paintings that dominate the text and fail to interpret the power of the ballet.

A handful of single illustrated folk-tales that reflect Canadian rather than European culture are mainly drawn from the rich heritage of native Indian and Inuit legends. Exceptions are the pioneer subject matter and transmuted old-world cultural imagery in Canada's first single illustrated folktale, *The Princess of Tomboso*, and later, *Simon and the Golden Sword* (1976), both complemented by Frank Newfeld's stylish art. The noodlehead tale of a pioneer simpleton in Carole Spray's retelling of *The Mare's Egg* (1981) has a Washington Irving–like tone and satirical illustrations by Kim La Fave that are reminiscent of Arthur Rackham's drollery and exquisite draughtsmanship. Other local immigrant legends and tall tales rooted in a regional story-teller's voice and sense of place include Joan Finnigan's musical tall tale of the Ottawa Valley—the saga of Joseph Montferrand, the giant lumberjack, in *Look! the Land is Growing Giants: A Very Canadian Legend* (1983), illustrated with Richard Pelham's witty pencil sketches. Joyce Barkhouse's *The Witch of Port LaJoye* (1983) is a Prince Edward Island and Micmac-Indian legend of eighteenth-century French-Canadian/Indian conflict and romance, illustrated in shimmering, mysterious watercolours by Daphne Irving.

Garnet Hewitt's retelling of, and Heather Woodall's illustrations for, the shamanistic Inuit legend *Ytek and the Arctic Orchid* (1981) return to the roots of Inuit culture. Hewitt's interpretation of the tale explores psychological realism within the tradition of the heroic legend. In parallel fashion, the pictures unite traditional visual motifs with contemporary graphic design.

But it is Elizabeth Cleaver whose illustrations stand for cultural transmission and continuity in her series of Indian legends created in collaboration with William Toye, whose laconic retellings are elegantly spare and concise. Cleaver's sensitivity to, and understanding of, the psychological patterns and innate drama in native legend imbue her interpretations with an emotional resonance beyond the surface story. In an unusual and innovative change in style, the artist who inaugurated Canadian full-colour book illustration in 1967 with *The Wind Has Wings: Poems from Canada* explored the rich potential of black and white in the shadow-puppet silhouettes for her final work, *The Enchanted Caribou* (1985). Like *Ytek and the Arctic Orchid*, this haunting Inuit legend tells a story of magical transformation and shamanism. In melodic prose that incorporates sacred chants and magical incantations, Cleaver recounts the enchantment of an Inuit maiden who is transformed into a white caribou and then back into a woman. This theme continues the sub-texts of metamorphosis and symbolic death and rebirth developed by Cleaver in earlier works such as *The Loon's Necklace* (1977), *The Fire Stealer* (1979), and *Petrouchka*. And, as in *Petrouchka*, her use of the semi-abstract puppet shapes provides a metaphorical distancing of the story: the book becomes a stage, a theatre for the enactment of archetypal drama. Fog, dream, and vision are crucial elements of the legend, and the photographs of black and white cut-out shadow puppets behind a lighted screen appear to move in and out of focus, creating the illusion of shrouded fog and magical transformation. The shadowy mists of the barren arctic tundra evoke a mythic, sacred time. A visual magic occurs on the page as the shape-shifting figures dematerialize and are transformed, slipping in and out of gauzy shadows. This poignant story, true to the stark nature of Inuit myth, rests upon a misty void, and it is the story-teller–artist's faith in human love that redeems this vision of the terrible frailty of human existence.

Among all these Canadian picture-book editions of folklore and legend there is no illustrated version of 'Cinderella', except for the pop-art collage pastiche illustrated by Alan Suddon, with its satirical adult commentary on the politics and society of the 1960s. But it is ironic that there is no Canadian version of 'Cinderella' that seriously interprets this most ancient and archetypal folk-tale, for this is the tale that best typifies the Canadian picture-book industry. Once the ignored and scorned step-child, the Canadian picture-book has, in the last decade, come of age. It has claimed its inheritance, adapting international trends in style and content to the Canadian experience. And it now occupies a significant position in the world family of Canadian and international children's literature.

ALDERSON, SUE ANN. *Bonnie McSmithers, You're Driving Me Dithers*. Illustrations by Fiona Garrick. Edmonton, Tree Frog, 1974, cloth (O.P.), paper.

ANDERSEN, HANS CHRISTIAN. *The Little Mermaid*. Retold by Margaret Crawford Maloney. Illustrated by Laszlo Gal. Toronto/London, Methuen, 1983, cloth.

ANDREWS, JAN. *Very Last First Time*. Illustrated by Ian Wallace. Vancouver/Toronto, Douglas, 1985, cloth (A Groundwood Book)

ANFOUSSE, GINETTE. *My Friend Pichou*. Translated by Mayer Romaner. Illustrated by the author. Toronto, New Canada, 1978, paper (My Friend Pichou) (First published in French, 1976)

ASCH, FRANK. *I Can Blink*. Illustrated by the author. Toronto, Kids Can, 1985, paper.

_____. *I Can Roar*. Illustrated by the author. Toronto, Kids Can, 1985, paper.

ASKA, WARABÉ. *Who Goes to the Park*. Illustrated by the author. Montreal, Tundra, 1984, cloth; 1986, paper.

ASSATHIANY, SYLVIE AND LOUISE PELLETIER. *Grandma's Visit*. Illustrated by Philippe Béha. Toronto, Lorimer, 1985, boards (Tot-Books) (First published in French, 1983)

ATWOOD, MARGARET AND JOYCE BARKHOUSE. *Anna's Pet*. Illustrated by Ann Blades. Toronto, Lorimer, 1980, cloth; 1986, paper (Kids of Canada)

BARKHOUSE, JOYCE. *The Witch of Port LaJoye*. Illustrated by Daphne Irving. Charlottetown, Ragweed, 1983, paper.

BÉHA, PHILIPPE. *Getting Dressed*. Illustrated by the author. Toronto, Lorimer, 1985, boards (Jumblebooks) (First published in French, 1985)

BLADES, ANN. *A Boy of Taché*. Illustrated by the author. Montreal, Tundra, 1973, cloth; 1984, cloth, paper.

_____. *By the Sea: An Alphabet Book*. Illustrated by the author. Toronto, Kids Can, 1985, cloth, paper.

_____. *Mary of Mile 18*. Illustrated by the author. Montreal, Tundra, 1971, cloth; 1984, cloth, paper.

BODGER, JOAN. *Belinda's Ball*. Illustrated by Mark Thurman. Toronto, Oxford, 1981, cloth.

CARRIER, ROCH. *The Hockey Sweater*. Translated by Sheila Fischman. Illustrations by Sheldon Cohen. Montreal, Tundra, 1984, cloth; 1985, paper.

CHASE, EDITH NEWLIN. *The New Baby Calf*. Illustrated by Barbara Reid. New York/Toronto, Scholastic, 1984, cloth, paper.

CHISLETT, GAIL. *The Rude Visitors*. Art by Barbara Di Lella. Toronto, Annick, 1984, cloth, paper (Annick Toddler Series)

CLEAVER, ELIZABETH. *ABC*. Illustrated by the author. Toronto/Oxford, Oxford, 1984, cloth.

_____. *The Enchanted Caribou*. Illustrated by the author. Toronto/Oxford, Oxford, 1985, cloth.

_____. *The Miraculous Hind: A Hungarian Legend*. Illustrated by the author. Toronto, Holt, 1973, cloth (O.P.)

_____. *Petrouchka*. Adapted from Igor Stravinsky and Alexandre Benois. Illustrated by the author. Toronto, Macmillan, 1980, cloth.

CLIMO, LINDEE. *Chester's Barn*. Illustrated by the author. Montreal, Tundra, 1982, cloth; 1983, paper.

DE ROUSSAN, JACQUES. *Beyond the Sun/Au-Dèla du Soleil*. Illustrated by the author. Montreal, Tundra, 1972, cloth (O.P.); 1977, cloth.

_____. *If I Came from Mars/Si J'Étais Martien*. Illustrated by the author. Montreal, Tundra, 1977, cloth.

DEWDNEY, SELWYN. *The Hungry Time*. Illustrated by Olena Kassian. Toronto, Lorimer, 1980, cloth; 1986, paper (Kids of Canada)

DOWNIE, MARY ALICE. *The Last Ship*. Illustrated by Lissa Calvert. Toronto, PMA, 1980, cloth (Northern Lights)

DOWNIE, MARY ALICE AND BARBARA ROBERTSON, comps. *The New Wind Has Wings: Poems from Canada*. Illustrated by Elizabeth Cleaver. Toronto/Oxford, Oxford, 1984, cloth, paper.

_____. *The Wind Has Wings: Poems from Canada*. Illustrated by Elizabeth Cleaver. Toronto, Oxford, 1968, cloth (O.P.); 1978, paper (O.P.); Rev. edn under title: *The New Wind Has Wings: Poems from Canada*. 1984, cloth, paper.

EYVINDSON, PETER. *Kyle's Bath*. Illustrated by Wendy Wolsak. Winnipeg, Pemmican, 1984, paper.

FAIRFIELD, LESLEY. *Let's Go/Allons-y* Illustrated by the author. Toronto, Kids Can, 1983, paper (Bilingual Word Books)

FINNIGAN, JOAN. *Look! The Land is Growing Giants: A Very Canadian Legend*. Drawings by Richard Pelham. Montreal, Tundra, 1983, cloth.

GAGNON, CÉCILE. *Snowfeather*. Translated by Valerie Hepburn Craig. Illustrated by the author. Toronto, Lorimer, 1981, cloth, paper (First published in French, 1980)

GALLOWAY, PRISCILLA. *When You Were Little and I Was Big*. Illustrations by Heather Collins. Toronto, Annick, 1984, cloth, paper (Annick Toddler Series)

GAY, MARIE-LOUISE. *The Garden*. Illustrated by the author. Toronto, Lorimer, 1985, boards (Little Big Books) (First published in French, 1985)

GILMAN, PHOEBE. *The Balloon Tree*. Illustrated by the author. Richmond Hill, Ont., North Winds, 1984, cloth.

HAMILTON, MARY. *The Sky Caribou*. Illustrated by Debi Perna. Toronto, PMA, 1980, cloth (Northern Lights)

HARRISON, TED. *Children of the Yukon*. Illustrated by the author. Montreal, Tundra, 1977, cloth; 1984, paper.

_____. *A Northern Alphabet*. Illustrated by the author. Montreal, Tundra, 1982, cloth.

HEARN, EMILY. *Good Morning Franny, Good Night Franny*. Illustrations by Mark Thurman. Toronto, Women's Press, 1984, paper.

_____. *Woosh! I Hear a Sound*. Design and illustration by Heather Collins. Toronto, Annick, 1983, cloth, paper (Polka-Dot Door Books); 1985, paper (Annikin)

HEIDBREDER, ROBERT. *Don't Eat Spiders*. Pictures by Karen Patkau. Toronto/Oxford, Oxford, 1985, cloth.

HERTZ, GRETE JANUS. *The Yellow House*. Illustrations by Iben Clante. Toronto, Annick, 1982, cloth (First published in Danish, 1973)

HEWITT, GARNET. *Ytek and the Arctic Orchid: An Inuit Legend*. Illustrations by Heather Woodall. Vancouver/Toronto, Douglas, 1981, cloth (O.P.); 1983, paper.

HOFFMANN, E.T.A. *The Nutcracker*. Retold by Veronica Tennant. Illustrated by Toller Cranston. Toronto, M & S, 1985, cloth.

KHALSA, DAYAL KAUR. *Baabee 1: Here's Baabee*. Illustrated by the author. Montreal, Tundra, 1983, boards (The Baabee Books, Series I)

_____. *Happy Birthday, Baabee*. Illustrated by the author. Montreal, Tundra, 1984, boards (The Baabee Books, Series III)

KOVALSKI, MARYANN. *Brenda and Edward*. Illustrated by the author. Toronto, Kids Can, 1984, cloth, paper.

KRONBY, MADELINE. *A Secret in My Pocket*. Illustrated by Anna Vojtech. Toronto, Magook, 1977, cloth (O.P.), paper (O.P.) (A Magook Book)

KURELEK, WILLIAM. *Lumberjack*. Illustrated by the author. Montreal, Tundra, 1974, cloth; 1977, paper.

_____. *A Northern Nativity: Christmas Dreams of a Prairie Boy*. Montreal, Tundra, 1976, cloth; 1984, paper.

_____. *A Prairie Boy's Summer*. Illustrated by the author. Montreal, Tundra, 1975, cloth; 1984, paper.

_____. *A Prairie Boy's Winter*. Illustrated by the author. Montreal, Tundra, 1973, cloth; 1984, paper.

LAURENCE, MARGARET. *Six Darn Cows*. Illustrated by Ann Blades. Toronto, Lorimer, 1979, cloth; 1986, paper (Kids of Canada)

LEE, DENNIS. *Lizzy's Lion*. Illustrated by Marie-Louise Gay. Toronto, Stoddart, 1984, cloth.

LEMIEUX, MICHÈLE. *What Is That Noise?* Illustrated by the author. London, Methuen, 1984, cloth.

LIM, JOHN. *At Grandmother's House*. Illustrated by the author. Montreal, Tundra, 1977, cloth; 1984, paper.

_____. *Merchants of the Mysterious East*. Illustrated by the author. Montreal, Tundra, 1981, cloth (Children's Books as Works of Art)

LIM, SING. *West Coast Chinese Boy*. Illustrated by the author. Montreal, Tundra, 1979, cloth.

LUNN, JANET. *The Twelve Dancing Princesses*. Illustrated by Laszlo Gal. Toronto, Methuen, 1979, cloth.

MCSWEENEY, SUSANNE. *The Yellow Flag*. Illustrated by Brenda Clark. Toronto, PMA, 1980, cloth (Northern Lights)

MAY, DAVID C., ed. *Byron and His Balloon: An English-Chipewyan Counting Book*. Illustrated by the children of La Loche and friends. Edmonton, Tree Frog, 1984, cloth.

MOAK, ALLAN. *A Big City ABC*. Illustrated by the author. Montreal, Tundra, 1984, cloth (Children's Books as Works of Art)

MORGAN, ALLEN. *Christopher and the Dream Dragon*. Pictures by Brenda Clark. Toronto, Kids Can, 1984, paper (A Kids-Can-Read Picture Book)

_____. *Christopher and the Elevator Closet*. Pictures by Franklin Hammond. Toronto, Kids Can, 1982, cloth, paper (O.P.) (Kids-Can-Read)

_____. *Matthew and the Midnight Tow Truck*. Art by Michael Martchenko. Toronto, Annick, 1984, cloth, paper (Matthew's Midnight Adventure Series)

_____. *Matthew and the Midnight Turkeys*. Art by Michael Marchenko. Toronto, Annick, 1985, cloth, paper (Matthew's Midnight Adventure Series)

_____. *Molly and Mr Maloney*. Pictures by Maryann Kovalski. Toronto, Kids Can, 1982, cloth (O.P.), paper (Kids-Can-Read)

_____. *Sadie and the Snowman*. Illustrated by Brenda Clark. Toronto, Kids Can, 1985, cloth, paper.

MULLER, ROBIN. *Mollie Whuppie and the Giant*. Illustrated by the author. Richmond Hill, Ont., North Winds, 1982, cloth; Richmond Hill, Ont., Scholastic-TAB, 1983, paper.

_____. *The Sorcerer's Apprentice*. Illustrated by the author. Toronto, Kids Can, 1985, cloth, paper.

_____. *Tatterhood*. Illustrated by the author. Richmond Hill, Ont., North Winds, 1984, cloth; Richmond Hill, Ont., Scholastic-TAB, 1984, paper.

MUNSCH, ROBERT N. *Mortimer*. Illustrations by Michael Martchenko. Toronto, Annick, 1983, paper (Annikin); Rev. edn, 1985, cloth, paper (Munsch for Kids)

_____. *Murmel, Murmel, Murmel*. Art by Michael Martchenko. Toronto, Annick, 1982, cloth, paper (Munsch for Kids)

_____. *The Paper Bag Princess*. Illustrations by Michael Martchenko. Toronto, Annick, 1980, cloth, paper (Munsch for Kids); 1981, paper (Annikin)

_____. *Thomas' Snowsuit*. Art by Michael Martchenko. Toronto, Annick, 1985, cloth, paper (Munsch for Kids)

MUNSIL, JANET. *Dinner at Auntie Rose's*. Art by Scot Ritchie. Toronto, Annick, 1984, cloth, paper.

NEWFELD, FRANK. *The Princess of Tomboso: A Fairy-Tale in Pictures*. Based on the story collected by Marius Barbeau and retold by Michael Hornyansky in *The Golden Phoenix*. Illustrated by the author. Toronto, Oxford, 1960, cloth (O.P.)

NEWFELD, FRANK [and William Toye]. *Simon and the Golden Sword*. Illustrated by Frank Newfeld. Toronto, Oxford, 1976, cloth (O.P.)

PARÉ, ROGER. *The Annick ABC Activity Set*. Based on an original idea by Roger Paré and Christine L'Heureux. Illustrated by the author. Toronto, Annick, 1985.

_____. *A Friend Like You*. Illustrated by the author. Toronto, Annick, 1984, cloth, paper (First published in French, 1983)

PASTERNAK, CAROL AND ALLEN SUTTERFIELD. *Stone Soup*. Illustrated by Hedy Campbell. Toronto, Women's Educational Press, 1974, cloth (O.P.), paper.

PERRAULT, CHARLES AND ALAN SUDDON (adapter). *Cinderella*. Including a French translation of the text by Claude Aubry. Illustrated by Alan Suddon. Ottawa, Oberon, 1969, cloth.

PITSEOLAK, PETER. *Peter Pitseolak's Escape from Death*. Introduced and edited by Dorothy Eber. Drawings by the author. Toronto, M & S, 1977, paper.

POULIN, STÉPHANE. *Ah! Belle Cité!/A Beautiful City ABC*. Illustrated by the author. Montreal, Tundra, 1985, cloth.

PRICE, MATHEW. *Peekaboo!* Illustrated by Jean Claverie. Richmond Hill, Ont., Irwin, 1985, boards.

RAWLYK, GEORGE. *Streets of Gold*. Illustrated by Leoung O'Young. Toronto, PMA, 1980, cloth (Northern Lights)

ROY, GABRIELLE. *Cliptail*. Translated by Alan Brown. Illustrated by François Olivier. Toronto, M & S, 1980, paper (First published in French, 1979)

SCHAFFER, MARION. *I Love My Cat!/J'Aime Mon Chat!* Illustrations by Kathy Vanderlinden. Toronto, Kids Can, 1980, paper (O.P.)

SINGER, YVONNE. *Little-Miss-Yes-Miss*. Illustrated by Angela Wood. Toronto, Kids Can, 1976, paper (O.P.)

SPRAY, CAROLE. *The Mare's Egg: A New World Folk Tale*. Afterword by Margaret Atwood. Illustrated by Kim La Fave. Camden East, Ont., Camden, 1981, cloth, paper.

STINSON, KATHY. *Big or Little?* Art by Robin Baird Lewis. Toronto, Annick, 1983, cloth, paper (Annick Toddler Series); 1985, paper (Annikin)

_____. *Mom and Dad Don't Live Together Any More*. Illustrations by Nancy Lou Reynolds. Toronto, Annick, 1984, cloth, paper

_____. *Red is Best*. Art by Robin Baird Lewis. Toronto, Annick, 1982, cloth, paper (Annick Toddler Series)

STRATFORD, PHILIP. *Olive: A Dog/Un Chien*. Illustrated by the author. Montreal, Tundra, 1976, paper (Mini Books for Mini Hands)

STREN, PATTI. *Hug Me*. Illustrated by the author. Toronto, Fitzhenry, 1977, cloth (O.P.); 1984, paper.

_____. *Sloan & Philamina; or, How to Make Friends with Your Lunch*. Illustrated by the author. Toronto, Clarke, 1979, cloth (O.P.)

SWAINSON, DONALD AND ELEANOR SWAINSON. *The Buffalo Hunt*. Illustrated by James Tughan. Toronto, PMA, 1980, cloth (Northern Lights)

TAKASHIMA, SHIZUYE. *A Child in Prison Camp*. Illustrated by the author. Montreal, Tundra, 1971, cloth; 1983, cloth, paper.

TANAKA, SHELLEY. *Michi's New Year*. Illustrated by Ron Berg. Toronto, PMA, 1980, cloth (Northern Lights)

TANOBE, MIYUKI. *Québec Je T'Aime/I Love You*. Illustrated by the author. Montreal, Tundra, 1976, cloth; 1984, paper.

TOYE, WILLIAM. *The Fire Stealer*. Pictures by Elizabeth Cleaver. Toronto/Oxford/New York, Oxford, 1979, cloth (O.P.); 1986, paper.

_____. *How Summer Came to Canada*. Pictures by Elizabeth Cleaver. Toronto, Oxford, 1969, cloth (O.P.); 1978, paper.

_____. *The Loon's Necklace*. Pictures by Elizabeth Cleaver. Toronto/Oxford/New York, Oxford, 1977, cloth.

_____. *The Mountain Goats of Temlaham*. Pictures by Elizabeth Cleaver. Toronto, Oxford, 1969, cloth (O.P.), paper.

VINCENT, FELIX. *Catlands/Pays des Chats*. Illustrated by the author. Montreal, Tundra, 1977, cloth.

VON KÖNIGSLÖW, ANDREA WAYNE. *Toilet Tales*. Illustrated by the author. Toronto, Annick, 1985, cloth, paper (Annick Toddler Series)

WALLACE, IAN. *Chin Chiang and the Dragon's Dance*. Illustrated by the author. Vancouver/Toronto, Douglas, 1984, cloth (A Groundwood Book)

WALLACE, IAN AND ANGELA WOOD. *The Sandwich*. Toronto, Kids Can, 1975, paper (O.P.); Rev. edn, 1985, paper.

WATERTON, BETTY. *Pettranella*. Illustrations by Ann Blades. Vancouver, Douglas, 1980, cloth.

_____. *A Salmon for Simon*. Illustrations by Ann Blades. Vancouver, Douglas, 1978, cloth; Richmond Hill, Ont., Scholastic-TAB, 1986, paper.

WHEELER, BERNELDA. *I Can't Have Bannock, but the Beaver Has a Dam*. Illustrated by Herman Bekkering. Winnipeg, Pemmican, 1984, paper.

WILSON, BARBARA. *ABC et/ and 123*. Illustrations by Gisèle Daigle. Toronto, Porcépic, 1980, paper.

WOOD, ANGELA. *Kids Can Count*. Illustrated with photographs. Toronto, Kids Can, 1976, paper (O.P.)

WYNNE-JONES, TIM. *Zoom at Sea*. Pictures by Ken Nutt. Toronto/Vancouver, Douglas, 1983, cloth (A Groundwood Book)

_____. *Zoom Away*. Pictures by Ken Nutt. Toronto/Vancouver, Douglas, 1985, cloth (A Groundwood Book)

WYSE, ANNE AND ALEX WYSE, eds. *Alphabet Book*. Designed by Allan Fleming. Toronto, University of Toronto, 1968, paper (O.P.)

_____. *The One to Fifty Book*. Toronto, University of Toronto, 1973, paper (O.P.)

ZOLA, MEGUIDO. *Moving*. Illustrated by Victoria Cooper. London, MacRae, 1983, cloth (Blackbird Series)

ZOLA, MEGUIDO AND ANGELA DEREUME. *Nobody*. Illustrated by Wendy Wolsak. Winnipeg, Pemmican, 1983, paper.

3

FICTION

Canadian writers of children's fiction share with their counterparts around the world certain fundamentals of tone and style and conventions of form and content. Individual authors use these literary features in diverse ways and with varying degrees of originality. But common to most children's fiction are narrative interest, child protagonists, emphasis on dialogue and action, and directness and clarity of style and tone. Like the best children's fiction anywhere, the best Canadian children's fiction possesses a strong plot, deft characterization, vitality of language, and emotional depth—all in creative tension—and a narrator's voice that reverberates with both a personal and cultural accent.

Historically the imaginative core of Canadian children's fiction has been rooted in geographical awareness. The impact of the land is reflected in the standard genres of Canadian children's literature: the wild-animal story, the wilderness adventure and survival story, and historical fiction. Other categories of fiction were explored far less successfully or received minimal attention prior to 1975. The roster of genres and sub-genres in international children's fiction is broad and deep, ranging, in realism, from the domestic story of child and family life to historical fiction; and in fantasy, from the literary fairy-tale to science fiction. Although many of these literary territories are still only sparsely populated with Canadian titles, there has been a vigorous exploration of new genres, themes, and modes in the last decade. Out of the many new voices, a select number of writers have emerged who speak with coherence and integrity. Their stories convincingly express personal realities. They explore social worlds and illuminate inner dreams with insights derived from living in a particular country. Without being ethnocentric, this new literature joins with the old to give Canadian children a sense of belonging. It provides them with the ancient power of 'naming': the power to name and own, to identify imaginatively with a place and people—with a culture.

REALISTIC FICTION

Child-and-Family-Life Stories

In children's realistic fiction, the child-and-family-life story has a long and hallowed tradition. It forms the bulk of reading material for many intermediate child readers. It deals with their immediate interests and experiences: the domestic dramas and comedies of family, school, and holidays; friends, siblings, and pets; emotional discoveries and gradual maturing. These are novels of humour, incident, and characterization, and are often written with a simple clarity. Such titles as Louisa May Alcott's *Little Women* (1868), Eleanor Estes's *The Moffats* (1941), and Beverly Cleary's *Ramona the Pest* (1968) spawned many series that centred on a single child or group of siblings. In Canada the foremost representative of this genre is L.M. Montgomery's unofficial international diplomat: *Anne of Green Gables* (1908). Nearly three-quarters of a century later, Bernice Thurman Hunter, in her *Booky* series, forges a link with the Montgomery tradition. She has created in Booky an unforgettable character, a high-spirited imaginative girl, a writer-in-embryo who is as sympathetic and three-dimensional as Anne herself. The series consists of three episodic novels: *That Scatterbrain Booky* (1981), *With Love from Booky* (1983), and *As Ever, Booky* (1985). Because there is no real plot other than the chronicling of Booky's growth from ten-year old child to teenager, there is plenty of room, against the backdrop of colourful incident and family drama, for character development. Booky changes from an irrepressible, feisty, disaster-prone child to a thoughtful, sensitive adolescent.

Set in Toronto during the Depression, the stories are anchored in a very real time and place, as palpably and lovingly described as Montgomery's Prince Edward Island. Based on autobiographical experiences, the novels have a sensuous immediacy and authenticity. The painful daily life of the Depression is presented as a child would see it, through the solace of family warmth. But there is no nostalgic glow to the details of grim poverty, no sentimentality in Booky's friendship with a mentally handicapped boy, or her experience of her grandfather's death. Also documented in vignettes and scenes are the pleasures and humour of everyday life: night skating on frozen Grenadier Pond; summer visits to country relatives in Muskoka; losing a babysitting job for eating forbidden oranges.

The reality of Canada is emphasized in the bond of story and story creators across generations. In an episode drawn from the author's life, Booky, as a young teenager, does not dream of being another Anne of Green Gables, but of being a real writer. When she meets Anne's creator, L.M. Montgomery, they share a funny, difficult, not altogether inspiring tea. The freshness and lack of stereotyping in the characters are also felt in the natural language and dialogue. The first-person narrative is intimate in tone, colloquial, and concrete with 1930s diction. The narrator's voice remains that of a child, buoyant with humour and warmth, as Booky observes the foibles and feelings of the people who make up her world.

Other writers of domestic family stories have also set their narratives in the near past, with a specificity of incidental detail of time and place that brings those eras to life. Myra Paperny's *The Wooden People* (1976) describes small-town life in late 1920s Alberta; Jean Little's *From Anna* (1972) and its sequel, *Listen for the Singing* (1977), are set in Toronto at the outbreak of the Second World War. Both writers create stories rich with vignettes of characterization and action. Each work has a strong sub-plot with serious overtones— shadows of war, alienation, and family upheaval.

The Jewish children in *The Wooden People* are chronic outsiders, in constant movement from one new town to another. Lonely and isolated, they are in conflict with their overbearing, histrionic father. Turning for solace to the realm of play, they create an alternate world of imaginative force and healing. They gain authority and emotional power by making wooden marionettes and performing puppet shows.

Jean Little's Anna also lives in a disturbing, untrustworthy world, moving from threatening pre-war Germany to a new language, culture, and society in Canada. This burden is compounded by her visual handicap, which leaves her vulnerable and isolated. As she grows into maturity and self-confidence with the aid of new glasses and friends, Anna becomes an important member of her family. An intuitive healer, she delicately moves and adjusts the emotional strings of family relations during the strained war years, much as the Stein children in *The Wooden People* heal their family rifts by manipulating real marionettes. Possessing some of the emotional vigour of the *Booky* series, both works engage the reader's feelings.

It is interesting that these novels of the near past have more solidity than the recent episodic stories of contemporary children's daily routines. The attention to accurate detail required to root the novels of Little and Hunter in the authentic Toronto of earlier eras is missing from the glossed-over settings of many contemporary family stories.

Despite their flaws—such as unrealized characterization or setting—a small group of novels succeed in developing and sustaining a mood or plot. Betty Waterton's *Quincy Rumple* (1984) uses a light, slapstick touch in its presentation of an eccentric family's madcap adventures and follies. Despite some awkwardness in style, this domestic comedy resembles a scaled-down 'Bagthorpe Saga' family farce by the droll British author Helen Cresswell. There are momentary lapses, also, in Patti Stren's *There's a Rainbow in My Closet* (1979), but the warmth and energy override some stereotypical characterization. Stren's narrative recounts young Emma's relationship with her grandmother and Emma's growth as an artist. The rather heavy-handed sentimentality is alleviated by the intimate portrayal of Emma's creative life and by her graceful, witty cartoon drawings and notes.

Claire Mackay's *The Minerva Program* (1984) combines a domestic story of a Toronto black family with a credible computer mystery. And Sue Ann Alderson's *The Not Impossible Summer* (1983) evokes the shimmery atmosphere of British Columbia's Gulf Islands. In the tradition of the holiday story, it details a young adolescent's summer of personal discovery as she teaches an older woman to read, makes friends, and begins to define her own world.

School Stories

The school story is another sub-genre of domestic realism that has been explored in Canada in the last decade, from farcical satire to serious study of the closed, microcosmic society of a boarding school.

Gordon Korman's boys' boarding school series, beginning with *This Can't Be Happening at Macdonald Hall!* (1978), provides the light, popular literature of slapstick farce and stereotypical antics that finds a parallel in the unrelenting action and minimal characterization of Eric Wilson's mysteries designed for reluctant readers.

The more serious approach to the school story is combined, in Veronica Tennant's *On Stage, Please* (1977), with an accurate rendering of the romance and drudgery of the world of ballet. Daily life in a residential Toronto ballet school is chock-full of Arthur Ransome–style details of how to master a craft, art, or skill. The insider's perspective on backstage life, as in *Ballet Shoes* (1936) by the British author Noel Streatfield, will satisfy the ballet *aficionado*'s hunger for specific detail, though the flatness of character and lack of narrative depth limit the book's power.

Another family and school story that centres on dance as a metaphor for personal magic and grace is Florence McNeil's freshly executed *Miss P. and Me* (1982). Narrated in the dryly witty, first-person voice of the younger adolescent novel, this story of Jane's grade eight year in a Catholic school maintains a tension between ironic humour and emotional subtlety. Its religious-school atmosphere, deft characterization of teachers and students, and wry satire on contemporary society recall the American M.E. Kerr's *Is That You, Miss Blue* (1975). Similar, also, are the poignant shifts in the teenage protagonist's perceptions of an eccentric dance teacher—from hero worship to intolerance to compassion. McNeil is an accomplished poet, and Jane's diary entries and poems, which reveal her growth as a writer, provide quiet, emotional relief to the stormy plot line of her growth into maturity as her lack of co-ordination destroys her dream of becoming a dancer. Her cruel revenge on her teacher is followed by guilt, contrition, and an understanding of the differences among human beings. The story's emotional conflict is leavened and resolved with humour and psychological insight.

Animal Stories

A traditional sub-plot of domestic fiction is the child-and-pet story, which provides scope for themes of emotional empathy and friendship, as well as a good measure of humorous incident, as in Farley Mowat's

Owls in the Family (1961). British author Philippa Pearce's *A Dog So Small* (1962) uses the pet-and-child relationship as a subtle metaphor for a child's obsessive internalization of loneliness. In Pearce's work the dog is a child's fantasy creation, existing only in the mind. But in Jean Little's *Lost and Found* (1985), which reinterprets the lost-pet convention as a novel of characterization and emotional growth for the younger reader, the dog and the child's loneliness are both real. Simply written with an economy that conveys much psychological nuance, the narrative concerns young Lucy's adjustment to a new neighbourhood, her grief for lost friends, and her vulnerable love for a runaway stray dog. The small events that loom poignantly large in a young life are given the dignity they deserve and are never sentimentalized. Both Lucy and her dog are lost, and both must be found—the dog by his original master and Lucy by finding a sense of belonging in her new home. The sharing of Lucy's emotional life, her intense feelings and maturing perceptions make this a rare and comforting book for the Beverly Cleary age group.

Distinct from the pet story are Canadian naturalistic wild-animal stories like those of Ernest Thompson Seton and Charles G.D. Roberts, which have almost disappeared in contemporary Canadian writing. The focus on animal life appears to have shifted in the last decade to the realm of non-fiction in the form of full-colour, photographic story-essays, such as those created by *OWL Magazine* in the 'Owl's True-Life Adventure Series', or the amateur naturalist's or veterinarian's reminiscences, like *Granny's Gang* (1984), Katherine McKeever's personal anecdotes about life in her refuge for owls. Quite different in tone from Little, McKeever, and the early writers is Gabrielle Roy's *Cliptail* (1980), a picture-storybook for beginning readers, translated with some charm from the original French. Roy uses a chatty, kitchen-table story-teller's voice to speak directly to the reader. In a warm French-Canadian tone, the narrator relates the country drama of a resourceful farm cat determined to defend her kittens.

Social Realism

The relative stability of the domestic child-and-family-life novel was unsettled in the 1960s and 1970s by a tumultuous wave of new realism that originated in the United States. Canadian children's realistic fiction did not really exhibit any evident response to the new literature's sharply contemporary, relevant themes until the late 1970s. The content of social realism—the candid treatment of psychological and emotional problems and contemporary social issues—has finally permeated Canadian realistic fiction. But most Canadian writers of the new realism seem to have skipped the phase of the banal, one-dimensional, taboo-breaking problem novel.

One series in this mode of social realism, 'The Adventure in Canada Series', is scrupulous in educational intent but uneven in execution and narrative control. Devoted to regional and ethnic representation of contemporary Canadian children's lives, this publishing project shows older children entering their teenage quest for identity against the background of the multicultural mosaic. Foreground issues, such as coping with discrimination, assimilation, divorce, parent-child conflict, and alienation often dominate the plot and dwarf the characters. Only a handful of these titles avoid the dullness of well-meaning but heavy-handed didacticism; they succeed by revealing a culture or place from the inside, rather than by describing it from the outside. Gloria Montero's *The Summer the Whales Sang* (1985) and Elizabeth Brochmann's *Nobody Asked Me* (1984) are novels in this series that use the settings of Labrador and Vancouver Island, respectively, as integral elements. The sense of place helps to define the emotional tone of these stories of family tension and romance. In both, the writing comes alive in the impressionistic and poetic imagery of the land-and-seascape, which is a focus for the young teenage girls' education of the heart.

Although not fully developed, the search for, and acceptance of, cultural origins is handled with some insight and drama in Monica Hughes's *My Name is Paula Popowich!* (1983) and Frances Duncan's *Kap-Sung Ferris* (1977). Both works provide vivid sketches of disturbed girls in search of their ethnic roots and both offer a concrete sense of Canadian urban life. Hughes's work unfortunately suffers from a surfeit of details of Polish-Canadian culture that are never fully integrated into the story or felt emotionally. Paul Yee sidesteps this pitfall in his collection of four linked short stories, *Teach Me to Fly, Skyfighter* (1983). Because of the structure of the short-story cycle, which offers quick, snap-shot perceptions and images, Yee's work conveys a collage impression of Vancouver's Chinatown and Strathcona district. The overlapping stories feature characters whose narratives reveal the strains among different cultural and immigrant groups and the enrichment they can offer each other.

Conscientious earnestness has marred some of Jean Little's earlier novels about disabled children in which the handicap often appears to dominate and restrict the unfolding of plot and character development. But this problem does not affect *Mama's Going to Buy You a Mockingbird* (1984), in which Little treats a family's reaction to the father's death with great insight. Like the American Katherine Paterson's *Bridge to Terabithia* (1977), Little's novel is not bibliotherapy, but a multi-dimensional look at the intricate web of family and friendship under the stress of a death. Paterson's work is emotionally charged, whereas Little's novel exhibits a restraint that seems significantly Canadian. In *Mama's Going to Buy You a Mockingbird* the action is primarily psychological, occurring in the mind of eleven-year-old Jeremy, who shares his father's acute perception and sensitivity. The plot is sequential and simply structured: Jeremy watches his father sicken and die; he grieves and binds his life to his mother and younger sister; he begins a new friendship with a girl who is an outsider at school but was a favourite pupil of his father; and he survives an uprooting move to a new home. Little's fresh dialogue reveals character well and conveys both the tensions and the restorative tenderness within the family. But the tone of her work is oblique and elliptical; an entire emotional life is implied in the silences and echoes between fragments of conversation, in the glances between characters, in all the myriad, fleeting moments of family life. A pattern of symbolic imagery—a series of images of birds and flight that reverberate with meaning—gives shape and texture to the story. The bird, as symbol of the spirit and the resurrection, weaves and dips throughout this narrative of death and rebirth. The images move from the title itself, to the bird-watching of father and son and the owl-carving that is the father's gift to Jeremy, to Dennis Lee's poem of the Ookpick's grace (a kind of Canadian Holy Ghost), and finally to Jeremy's winged flight at the book's end to wake his family to the healing, archetypal celebration of Christmas.

Young-Adult Fiction

As the novels move into the more complex terrain of young-adult fiction the exploration of contemporary social issues and themes of the new realism in children's fiction heats up. Before the late 1970s most Canadian writing for youth that featured young adult protagonists was firmly wedded to historical fiction and the outdoor-adventure and survival story. And to this day some of the best Canadian novels of adventure and historical fiction, as well as of fantasy and science fiction, have teenage protagonists. With the rise of social realism and the meteoric ascendency of the American young-adult novel in the 1960s and 1970s, Canadian writing slowly came to consider contemporary Canadian teenage life as a valid subject. There are still only a handful of novelists for young adults that focus on contemporary realities in this country, and, although their subject matter includes social problems, there has been little of the exploitation of sex and violence or trivialization of serious issues to be found in many of the one-dimensional, mass-market problem novels that constitute a significant factor in American young-adult literature. The Canadian approach is perhaps more conservative, less given to full-blown cynicism and despair, more emotionally honest, measured, and responsible.

The young-adult problem novel familiar in the writings of Americans Judy Blume and Norma Klein is typified by a first-person narrative, told in a colloquial, self-absorbed voice (raised in indefatigable lamentation over the real and imagined unfairnesses of life). There is little description or plot; the settings are bland and faceless urban centres. A wry, ironic wit may provide comic relief and social satire, as it does in the works of Americans Paul Zindel and M.E. Kerr. Canadian writers Gordon Korman in *Don't Care High* (1985) and Patti Stren in *I Was a 15-Year-Old Blimp* (1985) fall into this category. Neither work is set in Canada; both are set in New York but could take place in any large North American city. Decidedly in the stereotypical American style, these books use an interchangeable flat tone and voice. Stren deals seriously with the problem of bulimia; Korman with teenage apathy as extravagant farce; and though both books contain moments of sardonic wit, they lack characterization and insight.

By contrast, other Canadian writers for young adults employ very individualistic and identifiable voices in approaching sombre social issues or the all-consuming teenage struggle for independence and quest for identity. From the outport life of Newfoundland to the rolling Gatineaus, from the Alberta Rocky Mountain foothills to the islands of British Columbia, the best of the novelists are regional writers. Unlike the American young-adult writers, they create a localized reality, deeply rooted in both physical and emotional topography.

Even when the focus of plot and characterization is a limited, specific issue, these regional works treat the problem from a broader perspective than many of the American novels. One such example is Sandra Richmond's mature and graphic *Wheels for Walking* (1983), which piercingly conveys the shock, anger, and anguish suffered by a teenage girl after a car accident renders her quadraplegic. The narrator's slow and painful fight for wholeness is credible and touching.

Richmond's work is semi-autobiographical, which may account for much of its searing heat and emotional authenticity. Beatrice Culleton's *In Search of April Raintree* (1983) has a similar autobiographical tone of unrelenting honesty. The author, a Métis, recounts a contemporary urban tragedy: the story of two Métis sisters—from their childhood foster homes to the final suicide of one sister. The fictional structure is certainly flawed, but the details of abuse and rejection and the voices of fury and despair are deeply moving.

The terrible, unravelling loss of traditional native culture and its painstaking rediscovery in contemporary Indian life is also a theme repeated in several other Canadian young-adult novels. The best of these is Mary-Ellen Lang Collura's *Winners* (1984). Relationships are at the core of the book: between fifteen-year-old Jordy Threebears, orphaned and embittered veteran of eight years in foster homes, and his grandfather who leads a traditional life on the Alberta Blackfoot Indian Reserve; between Jordy and his new life on the reserve, his wild mare, and a blind girl he teaches to ride. Jordy's story is one of homecoming, literally and metaphorically, as he knits up the unravelling threads of his life. He explores his personal history while uncovering the mysteries surrounding his parents' deaths. Guided by his grandfather and a native elder and recluse, Jordy also experiences a personal binding into the fabric of his people's cultural history. And, finally, he receives a spirit guide in the form of a vision, a mythic Indian rider on a spirit horse who leads him home after he has been lost in a prairie blizzard and becomes Jordy's talisman in his search for identity. This mythic figure is introduced with a complete naturalism that adds an air of magic realism and spiritual depth to a work that is otherwise grounded in the actuality of prairie landscape and the rhythms of native speech patterns.

Unfortunately, the climax of *Winners* is somewhat melodramatic. A reliance on overly emotional resolutions also mars Marilyn Halvorson's *Cowboys Don't Cry* (1984) and *Let It Go* (1985), set, like *Winners*, in Western Alberta's rodeo and ranch country. Although lacking the delicate shading of Collura's writing, Halvorson's journalistic prose possesses the energetic directness and sentimentality of country and western music. The stories suffer, however, from clichéd characters and predictable plots. They have a naïve, melodramatic appeal much like the American S.E. Hinton's *Tex* (1979), which is also a contemporary horse-and-motorcycle western. These sagas of male teenage bonding, alienation from runaway and alcoholic parents, and the knife-play of teen warfare have more in common with Hinton's work than with the more mature voices of Collura, Kevin Major, and Brian Doyle.

Major and Doyle share top billing as the pre-eminent writers of contemporary young-adult literature in Canada. Their works possess integrity and literary skill while taking risks and pushing back the boundaries of the adolescent novel by experimenting with structure, style, and tone. Major set Canadian young-adult fiction on the national literary map in 1978 with the publication of his first novel, *Hold Fast*. A strong sense of place and loyalty to regional character imbue Major's works with the essence of Newfoundland: the people's hardy individualism; their devotion to the island, its unique customs and outport life, which are being eroded by urbanization and unemployment; and the islanders' colourful and graphic speech, which is earthy and rhythmic. Major's three novels—*Hold Fast* (1978), *Far From Shore* (1980), and *Thirty-Six Exposures* (1984)—form a coming-of-age trilogy about holding fast to the island's cultural values and accepting personal responsibility. They also show a progressive complexity and darkening vision. In each subsequent book, the male protagonists are older and the characters' problems more serious. And with each work the structure becomes more elaborate, reflecting—as in the writing of the American Robert Cormier—through more sophisticated structural devices, the author's increasing analysis of character, motivation, and perception. In *Hold Fast* Major uses the first-person confessional narrator familiar in the adolescent novel, which here conveys a real personal presence but offers a limited viewpoint. In contrast, *Far From Shore*'s multiple point of view enables the reader to envision empathetically—from the different perspectives of wife, son, and daughter—the disintegration of a family, the stresses of living with an unemployed, near-alcoholic father, and fifteen-year-old Chris's personal crisis. This extension of the usual perceptual restrictions of the adolescent novel continues in *Thirty-Six Exposures*. The work is composed of thirty-six short chapters that chronicle Lorne's final weeks before high-school graduation, his thoughts about the island's past and his future, his fragments of poetry and feelings about sex, his anger at authority and alienation from his family, and his reaction to his best friend's sudden death. As Lorne takes photographs of the island throughout the narrative, Major uses the camera as metaphor. The chapters are, in fact, the thirty-six exposures of the title—photographic shots that frame aesthetically and bring into focus people, events, landscape, and finally Lorne himself in a gallery of evanescent images. The multiple narratives, interior monologues, and fragmentary technique used in these novels emphasize the protagonists' and the reader's growing perception of life's multiple visions. The devices also have a distancing effect, reminding the reader that the work is deliberate artifice, something made.

For this reason *Far from Shore* and *Thirty-Six Exposures* lack the direct engagement with a character that the impassioned fourteen-year-old Michael offers in *Hold Fast*. His personal integrity, hatred of hypocrisy, and earthy idiom link him to those American progenitors of the adolescent-novel hero, Huckleberry Finn and Holden Caulfield. After his parents' death, Michael reacts with grief and rage towards his shattered world. Cut off from his loving grandfather, brother, and outport life of skidoos and squid-jigging, he struggles for emotional survival in his new, stifling suburban environment. He finally affirms his individuality and outport values by running away to the bush—a deserted winter campsite—for renewal.

Major's hard-hitting social realism shows an unflinching honesty in the colourful profanity used to reveal the characters' emotional confusion and tumult. His depiction of sexual attitudes—teenage males' emotional swings from personal desire to tenderness to brutish locker-room morality—is equally raw, paralleling the precarious balance developed in the novels between a quest for meaning and sheer survival. Life appears existential in Major's universe: the world is dangerous, often devastating; death is omnipresent—two parents, a grandfather, and a friend die; two protagonists narrowly escape death. There is little laughter or joy in these novels, but the characters, tenaciously rebuilding their lives through a vital sense of 'hold fast', cling with determination and pride to personal values and the cultural heritage of Newfoundland, and provide a measure of optimism.

Major's stark urgency is in direct contrast to the tone of Brian Doyle's work. Doyle's vision is also one of some moral ambiguity, but a gentle, luminous humour balances his probing of grim human dilemmas. His works are as experimental in their changes of tone and mood as Major's are in structure. The novels slide back and forth between the comic and the tragic mode with poignant shifts of sensibility. The existence of evil—cruelty, racism, and death—is redeemed by a vision of active human love and social and cosmic harmony.

Doyle's style is perfectly suited to the tragi-comic vision of love and death explored in his works. His prose can be as clean, laconic, and accessible as that of Hemingway. It can also shift to the confidential intimacy and artless rambling of the oral story-teller of tall tales. And the spare restraint of the first-person point of view carries a tight, suspenseful narrative that, though counterpoised by quietly lyrical soliloquies, never lapses into sentimentality.

In all his four novels—*Hey Dad!* (1978), *You Can Pick Me Up at Peggy's Cove* (1981), *Up to Low* (1982), and *Angel Square* (1984)— Doyle creates a highly coloured gallery of idiosyncratic, exaggerated characters, larger than life and legendary in community anecdote, as their names imply: Mean Hughie, The Hummer, Toe-Jam Laframboise. Carefully crafted running gags, outrageous cumulative jokes, and narrative extravagances, delivered in a quiet, deadpan tone, provide an ironic undercurrent and comic filigree to the serious text. The repeated tongue-in-cheek images and epithets act as the familiar tags of the oral story-teller, drawing the reader into the text as part of the family audience of shared, oral literature. Doyle's works inhabit a land between the novel and the folk saga, the family and community memoir that has been polished into localized legend. And, as in the folk world, children and young people are not segregated from adult characters and concerns. Doyle's fictional world is populated with three-dimensional characters; the protagonists' identities gradually unfold through dialogue, action, and interaction.

Doyle's first books—*Hey Dad!* and *You Can Pick Me Up at Peggy's*

Cove—are linked stories portraying the same family members. Promising examples of contemporary realistic fiction for younger adolescents, these books create deep emotional and psychological realism rather than surface social realism, and prefigure themes and images treated more maturely in the later *Up to Low* and *Angel Square*, which are also linked chronicles of an ongoing family saga. Recurring motifs and themes in all four books are: family life and its affections and tensions; odysseys—whether physical journeys through Canada or inner and psychological—as a context for emotional maturing; setting as an interpreter of history, culture, and intimator of the cosmic; and awareness of death and love.

Up to Low and *Angel Square*, which are set in the 1940s and 1950s, possess a more enduring resonance than Doyle's novels with more contemporary settings. In the Doyle tradition *Up to Low* is, on the surface, a rambling picaresque journey story. Set in the summer holidays of the 1950s, it is narrated by the teenaged Young Tommy, who travels with his father and the family friend Frank on a mock epic journey through the Gatineau Hills. Tommy falls in love with Baby Bridget, a girl with trillium-shaped eyes and a missing arm, and accompanies her in a gothic quest for her father, Mean Hughie, who is dying of cancer. Many of the images and motifs resemble those of Appalachian country ballads. The themes are large—love, death, hate, forgiveness, redemption—and they are interpreted with Doyle's unique blend of humour and pathos, spiced with a touch of the absurd that recalls Kurt Vonnegut. As original and daring as Doyle may be, his final reconciliatory denouements of reintegration, order, and hope are in the classic mode of comedy.

Angel Square is a prequel to *Up to Low* and is on the borderline between a children's and a young-adult novel. It shows Tommy as a younger boy in the Ottawa of 1945. The broad humour of earlier works has been toned down. Recurring characters from *Up to Low*, such as Aunt Dottie, who has a mania for cleanliness, and Frank, the alcoholic family friend, are more finely drawn, but the rich and odd panoply of human nature and character is still as joyously celebrated. The themes are as serious as in earlier works. Doyle treats the Jungian shadow side of human nature, as manifested in racial hatred and prejudice, with great sensitivity.

In a sense, the book is a mystery. Tommy, identifying with 'The

Shadow' of the 1940s radio program, sets out as a detective and crusader for justice to solve the mystery of a brutal anti-Semitic attack upon his best friend's father. What Tommy discovers is, in fact, the Jungian shadow: in the words of the radio Shadow, the evil that 'lurks in the hearts of men'. The ugly, murderous racism of the adult world is emphasized through its juxtaposition with an ironic foil: the frenzied, cartoon-like violence and rough-and-tumble play of the child world. A recurring motif is the mock heroic battles of the Jewish, Protestant, and French-Canadian kids of Ottawa's Lower-Town, who divide into ethnic and religious camps and, in the schoolyard tradition, gleefully pommel each other every day as they cross Angel Square to their respective parochial schools. The children, accepting of ethnic differences and untouched by hatred, remain fast friends. There are other mysteries, emotional and spiritual, in the book: the mystery of Tommy's mentally handicapped sister, of her Madonna-like face at the window, and of what she thinks and feels. The timelessness of the sister's emotions are linked to the mystery of the cosmos, which is intimated by Tommy's teacher and becomes concrete in the lunar eclipse. As in all of Doyle's writing, the sense of place and the contemplation of nature lead to a sensibility attuned to the infinite. A further mystery is that of the Catholic Mass: Tommy watches the criminal take Communion and considers the redemption of sinners. Doyle's complex vision, his loving tolerance of human nature, is conveyed in the resonant atmosphere of Christmas and is embodied in Tommy's unpretentious prayer for peace and love:

> A nice time:
> That's what I prayed for.
> The prayer might work, I thought.
> Or it might not.
> It was a mystery.

Prejudice also figures in two other novels that are set, like Doyle's work, in periods of near history. Mary Razzell's *Snow Apples* (1984) and John Craig's *Ain't Lookin'* (1983; originally entitled *Chappie and Me*, 1979) are written in the nostalgic tone of someone looking back from an adult perspective on the maze of adolescence—on its fresh vigour and painful moral ambiguities. *Snow Apples*, set in a British Columbia coastal village at the end of the Second World War, considers prejudice against women from the viewpoint of sixteen-year-old Sheila. The story recounts Sheila's angry, female rite of passage to maturity: her growth in understanding her embittered mother; her own sexual awakening and painful abortion; her conscious steps to independence. The impression of place is emotionally gripping.

Craig's *Ain't Lookin'*, based on incidents in the author's life, also explores prejudice from the viewpoint of an insider, but with a twist. In the Depression-era summer of 1939, a young white man in his late teens darkens his face with lampblack and joins an all-black baseball team touring small towns in Canada and the United States. Like the protagonist in John Howard Griffin's *Black Like Me* (1961), Joe finds that his new skin colour reveals to him another side of human life. He experiences the same humiliations and indignities as his black team-mates and shares a loving companionship with them. The mythology, poetry, and fellowship of baseball are conveyed as sweetly and strongly as in W.P. Kinsella's *Shoeless Joe* (1982).

Outdoor Adventure and Survival Stories

Most recent Canadian realistic fiction written for children considers the child within the context of an ordered universe— finding a place within the social units of family, friends, cultural traditions, school and other such institutions—and is usually urban in setting, dramatizing the protagonist's identity within a group and integration, in a larger sense, with society in general. Young-adult fiction, on the other hand, most often emphasizes the alienated outsider's separation from the social order, which is followed by a search for a personal, less cultural identity, climaxing in a coming-of-age ritual. In Canadian writing, this pattern of separation and quest is often depicted in the outdoor-adventure and wilderness-survival story. The opposition to society and the need for an isolated, primal setting to test the young-adult protagonist in a rite of passage pull the teenagers into the Canadian wilderness.

This is seen most strikingly in Monica Hughes's *Hunter in the Dark* (1982) and Jan Truss's *Jasmin* (1982). In both novels troubled adolescents run away into the Alberta bush, learn about emotional and physical survival, and experience an integration of the self. Sixteen-year-old Mike Rankin, in *Hunter in the Dark*, escapes to the wilderness to fulfil his dream of hunting the white-tailed deer. The classic rite-of-passage novel of young manhood often reverberates with the pattern of the hunt and the first victorious kill. Mike is not only the hunter; he is also the hunted, pursued by the horrible knowledge that he is dying of leukaemia. The hunter in the dark is death. But, as Mike faces his own dark fear of death, he chooses life in a desperate struggle for survival during a night of storm. And, in choosing not to kill the deer, he finally accepts the fact that life and death are irrevocably intertwined.

The effect of Hughes's cool, clear writing is more contemplative than the intense romanticism evoked in Truss's *Jasmin*. Here the protagonist is a runaway girl, fleeing from the unfair burden of adult responsibility in a large, chaotic, demanding family and from her fear of failing grade six. Inspired by a character in her favourite poem by Keats, Jasmin acts out the romantic fantasy of seeking solitude in the wilderness. As she makes the wilderness her home, the northern Alberta bush and its animal life come alive vividly. Jasmin's sense of self is strengthened by the healing power of nature and her discovery of an innate artistic talent: she models clay sculptures of the forest animals. But the wilderness is not only a source of mystical communion. It is also dangerous and life-threatening, and a more independent Jasmin returns to society to reconcile herself to her family and school life.

Like Mike Rankin, who is threatened by imminent death, Jasmin has a shadow companion in the dark—her retarded brother, Leroy, who runs away to look for his sister. Leroy's search parallels Jasmin's as she travels deep into her psyche to discover the artist who perceives the beauty and terror of animal life; he descends into his unconscious and becomes lost in a regression into dark, animal behaviour, not unlike that of the animals observed by Jasmin. The sister's reintegration with the social order is linked to her rescue of Leroy, who is also returned to the human community.

Very different from these deeply psychological survival stories in which the wilderness becomes a metaphor for the unconscious is the traditional outdoor-survival story as told by the prolific James Houston. Continuing in the straightforward mode of the turn-of-the-century boys' high adventure tale, Houston uses a raw, direct style that suggests journalistic reportage. His deep knowledge of the Canadian North imbues his novels with a powerful sense of the Arctic that has far more impact than the Alberta bush of Truss and Hughes. In Houston's geographical imagination the Arctic is not an abstraction of the Canadian consciousness but a character in its own right, a motivator of action, and a determinant of plot. Whether the setting is northern Quebec and Labrador, as in *River Runners* (1979), or the Baffin Island tundra of the trilogy composed of *Frozen Fire* (1977), *Black Diamonds* (1982), and *Ice Swords* (1985), the land is real, rugged, and treacherous and engages the protagonists in a struggle for survival and in a continuing love-hate relationship.

As indicated in the turn-of-the-century *Boy's Own Paper* tone of his subtitles—*A Tale of Courage*; *A Tale of Hardship and Bravery*; *A Search for Arctic Treasure*—Houston's themes are those of classic high adventure. Amplifying the rite-of-passage testing of the adolescent male under elemental conditions and perils, he creates heroic adventures of survival against wild animals, cold, and starvation, and harrowing searches for treasure. The treasure may be gold or oil, but it is usually a handicap to survival and is ultimately sacrificed in order to save human lives. The real treasure is found in the rewards of self-recognition and friendship.

In most of Houston's works since 1975 his protagonists are a pair of teenagers: a white boy from southern Canada and a native Indian or Inuit youth who initiates the newcomer into the beauty and danger of the land and into the aboriginal lore and traditions that teach the skills of living in harmony with nature. Houston's writing is usually based on factual incidents, but prior to 1975 many of his adventure narratives were set in a mythic past. In the last decade his writing has dramatized the contemporary clash of cultures in the North, the conflict between traditional ways of life and western attitudes and values, which intrude upon and often ravage the Arctic.

Despite Houston's crisp style and compelling pace, his novels—perhaps because they are genre fiction with little room for originality or psychological depth—are numbingly similar in plot and often schematic in characterization. His most moving and controlled narratives are not his young-adult works laden with Robinsonnade survival details, but his shorter, more sparely written works for younger children. An example is *Long Claws* (1981), a picture-storybook illustrated with Houston's own rounded, Eskimo carving-style drawings. Like his retellings of Inuit legends, this lean story about the journey of a brother and sister to find a frozen caribou that will save their family from starvation gains resonance from the folk pattern of two children on a survival quest and from the mythic element of a snow-owl spirit guide. The ancient Inuit animism of the grandfather, the children's stoicism and fortitude in the face of death, and the attack by a bear are all elements that recall the only fiction written by an Inuit, Markoosie's tragic *Harpoon of the Hunter* (1970). Houston abandons his journalistic style in his shorter works for a more polished, economical language of legend, similar to Markoosie's Inuit voice.

HISTORICAL FICTION

The survival-story genre has traditionally encompassed wilderness-survival adventures with historical settings. Although *Long Claws* is contemporary, it has a timeless aura and could have taken place at any stage of Inuit history. Historical survival stories, such as Jan Hudson's *Sweetgrass* (1984), are representative of the shift in Canadian children's historical fiction of the last decade. Earlier works usually elaborated, often with contrivance of fact, on familiar incidents of Canadian history or used history as a colourful backdrop for the rough-and-tumble adventures and daring deeds of historical romance. This approach continues today in Tony German's nineteenth-century series, which begins with *Tom Penny* (1977).

Stories of Social History

Rarely have writers for children created social history or explored the psychological temper of a period or the social fabric of a cultural group. The main international trend in recent children's historical fiction has been a shift from the romantic historical myths and heroic struggles of epoch-shaping historical figures and events to the social history of authors such as the British Leon Garfield and Hester Burton. The new low-keyed works of Canadian social history attempt to bring alive the milieu and mores of a particular era. When fully integrated with authentic social history, a survival story like *Sweetgrass* successfully combines taut, suspenseful narrative with the imaginative recreation of a particular era.

The realities of social history are a crucial element in Hudson's story of Sweetgrass, a fifteen-year-old Blackfoot Indian girl of the early nineteenth-century Canadian Prairies. Sweetgrass chafes against the restricted role of women in her native society. She comes to see that her life possibilities are circumscribed by the profound social changes brought about by contact with the Europeans. Compared to her grandmother, who enjoyed relative freedom in her youth, Sweetgrass finds her activities severely limited. Within this historical context, Hudson tells a story of survival and maturing to independence that has parallels in *Island of the Blue Dolphins* (1960), a Robinsonnade by the American Scott O'Dell. Like O'Dell's female protagonist, Sweetgrass must break tribal taboos and take responsibility for her ethics and decisions in order to ensure her family's survival. She puts aside her childhood needs and youthful dream of a husband to endure adult trials and tests. With self-reliance, ingenuity, and courage, she helps her family survive an attack by another tribe, winter starvation, and smallpox.

The best of Canadian historical fiction written for children before 1975 took its subject from the native experience. *Sweetgrass* follows in this tradition, except that, unlike Roderick Haig-Brown's *The Whale People* (1962) and other earlier titles, it has a female protagonist. *Sweetgrass* is as much a cultural rite of passage as earlier works with male protagonists, but it contains a more vivid revelation of the inner self. The rhythm and tone of the work are also more organic, feminine, and poetic. With all its taut drama, the story is told in slow, rhythmic prose and spare, sensuous imagery; and, framed within a single year, it reflects the changing prairie seasons and the women's endless cycle of physical labour.

The richly drawn, convincing world of *Sweetgrass* offers the reader ample opportunity to live inside another era. Despite the large number of historical narratives in Canadian children's literature before 1975, few have had any real impact. Most were overly serious and instructive non-fiction historical accounts disguised as fiction, or simplistically action-paced, stereotypical historical romances of raw adventure—neither of which produced a vibrant renewal of the past. Since 1975 an increasing number of writers of historical fiction have chosen not to sacrifice narrative energy to didactic purpose and have followed the way of the story-teller, shaping tales that are true psychologically as well as historically.

One such story-teller is Marianne Brandis, whose two companion volumes, *The Tinderbox* (1982) and *The Quarter-Pie Window* (1985), depict a young woman's life in the harsh pioneer society of rural Southern Ontario in the 1830s. Like Hudson, Brandis makes no revisionist attempts to alter historical attitudes to make them more palatable to contemporary views; the female protagonist's life is as restricted as that of Sweetgrass. The two novels chronicle devastating change and gradual maturing in the life of a young teenager, Emma Andersen. As in *Sweetgrass*, historical verisimilitude is achieved through an intricate web of surface and internal detail: the emotional rhythms of Emma's inner life echo the daily rhythms of endless physical work and seasonal cycles. Vignettes of rural life reveal the brutality and harshness of pioneer society and bush farming and the complexity of life itself, which is both cruel and regenerative. Emma reads eighteenth-century novels of coincidence and moral ambiguity, such as Richardson's *Pamela* (1741) and Fielding's *Tom Jones* (1749). Brandis's plots have a similar tone of romance and use similar conventions: the young, orphaned protagonist and the secretive, manipulative relatives; the movement from country to city on a quest for independence.

In the first book—in which Emma's family dies in a log-cabin fire—the action is internal, focusing on Emma's choices and decisions; the narrative is dense with introspection, memory, and grief. In the sequel Emma moves to York, where she works in drudgery at her aunt's hotel and attains a new maturity. Brandis's special achievement is neither in the slow-moving narrative nor in the subtle integration of social history with plot. Like Jane Austen's novels of social manners and fully realized characters, the works are most affecting in Emma's multi-faceted responses to events and her insight into human feelings, motivation, and behaviour. Appropriate imagery of vision and perception—eyes, glances, reflections, and windows—forms a resonant pattern. As in *Sweetgrass*, the reader experiences in the humanity of Emma's story the continuity of human perception and emotion. The tiny, historically accurate wood engravings by Gerard Brender à Brandis give a tangible sense of period to the novel.

The influence of social history has been pervasive. Even those Canadian writers of the last decade who continue to focus on specific historical events that determine the plot structure usually treat ordinary people's lives, rather than those of well-known historical or national figures. In so doing they address the formation of Canada's early national identity. Examples of this trend are Mary Beacock Fryer's episodic novel of the United Empire Loyalists, *Escape: Adventures of a Loyalist Family* (1976); a rough study of the War of 1812, Gregory Sass's *Redcoat* (1985); and Barbara Greenwood's *A Question of Loyalty* (1984), which dramatizes the Mackenzie Rebellion of 1837.

The current writers of social history display a rich diversity of setting, period, and people. They may focus on a particular cultural group, as Brenda Bellingham does in *Storm Child* (1985), a novel of nineteenth-century Métis life on the Canadian frontier; or they may dramatize political and economic realities and social issues, such as Canadian labour history, as Bill Freeman does in an uneven series on nineteenth-century working conditions (especially child labour) and the fight for unionization. The best of this series is *Harbour Thieves* (1984); its Dickensian overtones and dramatic story transcend the wooden stereotypes that tend to mar Freeman's writing.

A richer treatment of this new realism, which depicts social and moral issues previously ignored in historical fiction, is found in Marsha Hewitt and Claire Mackay's *One Proud Summer* (1981). Another narrative of labour history, it combines a dramatization of the bitter mill-worker's strike of 1946 at Valleyfield, Quebec—including its complex social associations with church and state—with the subtle, domestic drama of a mother–daughter–grandmother relationship. The authors avoid being doctrinaire or melodramatic; the moral relevance broadens from an important, but narrow, social issue into an exploration of human behaviour and feeling.

Almost all these works of social history are marked by a dependence on pedagogical apparatus perfectly designed for classroom use: appendices, glossaries, bibliographies, historical notes, and archival photographs abound. In England and the United States historical fiction published as trade books for children and young adults does not, on the whole, include such teaching materials. The Canadian trend appears to represent a real anxiety—that children here need more instruction in our history. But it also displays a misunderstanding of the power of historical fiction to speak for itself, to embody fact within a compelling narrative, and to convince the reader of Canadian history's reality and emotional significance.

Barbara Smucker's historical fiction rises above the lacklustre and the didactic. Her writing is simple and direct, and she has one major, recurring theme. *Underground to Canada* (1977) and *Days of Terror* (1979) are dramatic narratives of Canada's basic, elemental story: exodus and arrival. Writing of the movement from bondage to freedom—the story of leaving home and arriving in Canada—she chronicles the experiences of different racial and cultural groups: their flight from hardship and injustice and their journey to freedom in a new homeland. Smucker's stories and characters are representative of the immigrant experience in general, without being formulaic. Her writing is rooted in carefully researched, specific historical detail, her plots are full of conflict and tension, and her characters are flesh-and-blood individuals engaged in life-and-death struggles.

In *Underground to Canada*, Julilly does not represent all runaway black slaves. She is a real girl, escaping from the plantations of the American South to Canada via the Underground Railroad. The author writes with the restraint of the American Paula Fox in *Slave Dancer* (1973). Like Fox, Smucker lets the telling detail stand for the whole, without belabouring or exploiting the already horrific facts. Julilly is in emotional turmoil, but she perseveres with stoic determination. The drama of the hunt and pursuit and the endless yearning for freedom add page-turning suspense to this tale of personal courage.

Days of Terror describes a wave of Mennonite immigration to Canada from the southern Ukraine following violent persecution—pillage, starvation, killings—during the early years of the Russian Revolution. Unlike the subtle dramatization and assimilation of fact in *Underground to Canada*, the elaboration of Mennonite history and of culture and politics occurs in passages of explication that arrest the narrative. But, once again, Smucker captures the reader's imagination with the sheer dramatic tension in her presentation of ordinary people caught up in the sweeping changes of world history.

In these novels of escape to a new beginning, Canada is envisioned as a haven, an ideal of freedom. But the actual reality of adjustment to Canadian life is never described. The safe arrival in Canada and the settling in Ontario or Manitoba are anticlimactic because Canada is a symbol, never a fully realized setting. Only in Smucker's contemporary novel, *Amish Adventure* (1983), is an ethnic group shown as a living entity within the multicultural mosaic. Smucker delineates the problems of prejudice and isolation, the choices of living apart or adapting to a wider national culture.

Stories of Historical Romance and High Adventure

One work of historical fiction that dramatizes not only immigration but the difficult adjustment to the new land is Suzanne Martel's *The King's Daughter* (1980), translated from the French. Although the details of pioneer life in the New France of the 1670s are accurate and believable—providing an overview of society from the *voyageurs* and Indians to the remnants of French nobility—the total effect is not one of carefully documented social history, for this is a highly coloured historical romance. *The King's Daughter* is a saga of high adventure that incorporates many of the conventions, contrivances, and stereotypes of the Romantic novel, from Brontë's *Jane Eyre* (1847) to the Harlequin romance.

Jeanne Chatel is a high-spirited, imaginative eighteen-year-old orphan in a French convent who thrives on chivalric fantasies. One of the King's Daughters sent to New France as wives for the settlers, Jeanne arrives in an exotic land to marry, by accident, a domineering, brooding, Byronesque trapper. Romantic misunderstandings ensue and are ultimately resolved. The novel's structure is formulaic and the prose is, at times, hackneyed and marred by awkward anachronisms, but the vitality and personal heroism of the protagonist are engaging. Jeanne's intrepid adventures are the stuff of the *Boy's Own Paper*. The hardships of life in the wilderness are seen through Jeanne's eyes with a vision more true to twentieth-century than to seventeenth-century sensibilities, and they are interpreted with an odd mixture of accurate historicity and revisionism. The pioneer men are referred to as misogynist, for example, and Jeanne rebels against her husband's expectations that women be passive and obedient. However, this perspective on women's struggle for independence is juxtaposed with the depiction of the Iroquois as dirty, untrustworthy savages, which is probably truer to actual seventeenth-century opinion than Martel's depiction of rebellious womanhood. *The King's Daughter* is more a vigorous costume drama than convincing social history.

Other works in this category of high adventure include Ruth Nichols's *The Left-Handed Spirit* (1978), which tells a wildly imaginative, embroidered adventure saga. Set in the tenth century on the Silk Road, it creates an exotic atmosphere evocative of Marco Polo's travel memoirs.

Similarly, Joan Clark's *The Hand of Robin Squires* (1977) owes a debt to the absorbing drama of the high-adventure sea saga, and to Robert Louis Stevenson's *Treasure Island* (1883) in particular. The novel, inspired by the discovery of a mysterious severed hand in a shaft on Oak Island, Nova Scotia, is, in one sense, a mystery. Such elements as vividly characterized and grotesque pirate villains, an eighteenth-century mystery of buried treasure and cruel murder, and a young protagonist groping his way through a maze of treachery and evil recall the writing of both Stevenson and the British author Leon Garfield. The presence in the story of black slaves, used to build the treasure shaft, and the protagonist's anticipation of their certain death, add gravity and horror to the narrative. The protagonist's growth is one of ironic self-knowledge, as he looks back poignantly on his youthful naïvety.

FANTASY

The category of high adventure, in Canadian and international writing for children, occasionally features imaginative narrative elements that are plausible but border on the fantastic. True fantasy, however—classic epic fantasy of serious moral struggle between good and evil, set in fully realized Other Worlds—has never been a strength in Canadian writing for children. In Britain, fantasy writing is rooted in the soil of the European oral tradition, which draws upon a rich Celtic, Saxon, and Roman history and such national epic romances as the Arthurian legend, but in Canada the overpowering and alienating landscape and the lack of a folk tradition and history rooted in humanly hospitable places have provided arid ground for national epic fantasy. Even Canadian native Indian and Inuit myths and legends do not provide the sense of a localized, rooted heritage essential for the growth of fantasy; because they belong to the native peoples, their power is difficult to translate into the national imagination. No Canadian fantasist, not even Catherine Anthony Clark, has created a convincing new world based on native folklore, such as that found in the aboriginal *The Ice is Coming* trilogy (1977–1981) by Australian Patricia Wrightson.

As well as the classic, epic, mythic fantasy, the many other subgenres of fantasy fiction—from light domestic fantasy to science fiction—have been sparsely represented in Canadian children's literature. Very few titles of convincing literary and aesthetic power have emerged that offer refreshment and release or that are at home in the mythopoeic terrain of fantasy—the symbolic and psychological quest for the truths of the human spirit. There has been no real successor, since 1975, to Ruth Nichols or Catherine Anthony Clark, who attempted to integrate Canadian landscape or native myth with themes of classic fantasy in their works. Fantasists of the last decade who have tried to create logical and internally consistent secondary realities include William Pasnak, in his *In the City of the King* (1984), and Nancy-Lou Patterson, in *Apple Staff and Silver Crown* (1985). Though these promising fantasies display a poetic sensibility and a commitment to the tradition of high epic fantasy, they are both marred by a lack of narrative control and tension. Patterson provides a surfeit of extraneous mythic detail that drowns character and motivation, whereas Pasnak's writing suffers from a diffuse conception of the secondary world and an absence of exactitude and inner coherence.

Literary Fairy-tales and Fables

In the category of the literary fairy-tale and fable, which draws on folklore motifs and offers psychological or spiritual morals, the most delicately modulated creation in the last decade is Donn Kushner's *The Violin-Maker's Gift* (1980). Set in the French Pyrenees in the Napoleonic era, the story possesses some of the romantic and satirical atmosphere that we find in Hans Christian Andersen's nineteenth-century literary fairy-tales. The allegorical narrative of a poor violin-maker and a magical bird with a spellbinding song and an extraordinary, disconcerting habit of delivering oracular truths in human speech is poignantly told.

Equally successful is Antonine Maillet's finely crafted *Christopher Cartier of Hazelnut, Also Known as Bear* (1984), originally written in French. Maillet's Acadian fable is a tongue-in-cheek animal fantasy, sparkling with word-play and written in the French romantic tradition of Antoine de Saint-Exupéry's philosophical *The Little Prince* (1943). With delicate charm, Maillet creates a parable of friendship between the narrator, a writer living in an abandoned New Brunswick lighthouse, and an endearingly naïve, proud, obstreperous bear-cub given to boisterous scrapes, word-play and malapropisms. The narrator, like the pilot in *The Little Prince*, observes the bear-cub's moral and emotional education and comments on the nature of time and mutability. As in E.B. White's *Charlotte's Web* (1952), the glory of the natural world and the mystery of friendship are restorative, providing an enriched perception of ordinary life. And, as in *The Violin-Maker's Gift*, the poetic style and urbanity of the story result in an overall contemplative tone that, at times, has more adult than child appeal. Both books are gentle, perceptive, and romantically old-fashioned in the mode of European literary fairy-tales.

Light Fantasy

Perhaps the best-known Canadian fantasy is Mordecai Richler's *Jacob Two-Two Meets the Hooded Fang* (1975). Richler's work, which has an energetically raw, comic-book appeal, is an example of light, domestic, or nonsense fantasy; its broad satire possesses some of the bite that enlivens his adult novels. Set in England, the narrative recounts the adventures of a young boy who dreams he is tossed into the dungeons of Slimers' Isle, a children's prison, for insulting an adult. A sly variation of the Victorian childrens' cautionary tale, the story has much in common with the slapstick style and exaggerated farce of Roald Dahl's *Charlie and the Chocolate Factory* (1964), without that book's ambiguous and cruel overtones. And, like Swedish author Astrid Lindgren's *Pippi Longstocking* (1944), it is also a mock-heroic affirmation of children's autonomy in the face of their powerlessness in the adult world.

Time-Travel Fantasy

The most vigorous sub-genre in Canadian children's fantasy of the last decade has been the time-travel or time-slip category. Perhaps this is because the only true elements of fantasy and magic in the time-travel genre are movement across time and the talisman or plot device that precipitates the travel through time and space. And, considering Canadian children's writers' predilection for historical fiction, it is natural that they would be comfortable with a genre in which the time travel leads into historical fiction and dramatizes the daily life and customs of a particular period. The evocative power of the Canadian landscape and the innate drama of historical sites are also factors in many time-travel works. Setting often plays a crucial role. The child protagonist's sensitivity to the residual layers of time in a particular place may provide the emotional connection that links two eras and motivates the action. The themes explored in these works include the consoling power of memory, cultural identity in times of historical conflict, and the continuity of human values, family traditions, and heritage in the face of change.

For younger children, Margaret Laurence's picture-storybook *The Olden Days Coat* (1979) uses the device of an old winter coat found in a trunk to transport Sal, a ten-year-old girl, to a long-ago Christmas, where she meets her grandmother as a young girl. Both protagonist and reader experience the connection between life in the past and life in the present, as well as the potential empathy between generations. Without intense drama or conflict, the simply told story is a pastoral of rural Canadian winter, full of nostalgia for horse-drawn sleigh rides and family Christmases.

The protagonist in *The Olden Days Coat* is unhappy, depressed, and bored at the story's opening—a characterization common to many time-travel novels. Often the protagonists are lonely, disturbed, or confused by internal or external conflict in their lives. In such fine time-travel novels as *Tom's Midnight Garden* (1958) by the British author Philippa Pearce, and *Playing Beatie Bow* (1982) by the Australian Ruth Park, the protagonists' emotional turmoil precipitates their travel into another era, in which they become distanced from, and finally resolve, their inner conflict. This is also true of Janet Lunn's *The Root Cellar* (1981). Rose Larkin, a difficult, thorny twelve-year-old American girl, is a lonely orphan unused to close relationships, much like Mary Lennox in Frances Hodgson Burnett's *The Secret Garden* (1911), which is Rose's favourite book. After the death of her guardian grandmother, Rose comes to live with a large, boisterous family of unknown Canadian relatives in their decrepit old Ontario farmhouse. A protected city child, Rose cannot adjust to his new life; her misery and estrangement lead her to wander through the old house's root cellar into an era as metaphorically divided as her own heart—the time of the American Civil War.

There she finds companionship and understanding, leaving her self-absorption and taking the first step towards maturity. The path to maturity becomes a perilous journey to Washington, D.C., in search of a lost friend—a young Canadian who enlisted in the Union Army only to discover that the American conflict was not his war. Like the protagonist in Stephen Crane's *Red Badge of Courage* (1895), Rose bears witness to the grim horror of civil war. The emotional war in Rose's heart heals as she, like her friend, discovers a sense of kinship with people and place that overcomes her isolation. Even though Rose may always feel torn between two centuries and between her dual national identities, her loyalties have found a home in Hawthorn Bay, Ontario. The final Christmas scene of *The Root Cellar*, like that in Jean Little's *Mamma's Going to Buy You a Mockingbird*, evokes reconciliation, order, and harmony.

The ethical dilemma posed by conflicting loyalties in times of violent war is also a theme in O.R. Melling's *The Druid's Tune* (1983), although it is treated with less subtlety than is shown in Lunn's work. *The Druid's Tune* is notable for the vigour, humour, and inventiveness with which the author recounts the adventures of two Canadian teenagers who travel back in time to the ancient world of early Ireland, with its mythical warrior kings and queens, and epic heroes. The premise is exciting and the pace compelling, but the banal writing lacks the grandeur and dignity that have made the treatment of Celtic myth and prehistory by Briton Rosemary Sutcliff so credible and moving. The problem in *The Druid's Tune* appears to be its inconsistent mood and tone. The epic Ulster hero, Cuculann, changes from a morally ambiguous mythic figure to Cucuc, a comic bully; the violence slides from serious carnage to cartoon-like frenzy, undercutting the promising drama of the story.

Other works in this genre that are partially effective but lack scope and dimension are Barbara Smucker's *White Mist* (1985), an overly didactic narrative of two native Indian teenagers who witness the environmental destruction of Michigan's forests and lakes, and two fantasies of time travel set in the gold-rush town of Barkerville, B.C.—Ann Walsh's *Your Time, My Time* (1984) and Florence McNeil's *All Kinds of Magic* (1984). Karleen Bradford's *The Other Elizabeth* (1982) and Heather Kellerhals-Stewart's *Stuck Fast in Yesterday* (1983) convey the claustrophobia of being trapped in the past and losing one's identity, but, unfortunately, the motivation of character and conflict between the two epochs are never convincingly realized.

Supernatural and Psychological Fantasy

Another type of fantasy—one that is almost unclassifiable—is becoming prevalent in Canadian writing: a loose amalgam of magic realism and the supernatural, of ghost stories and psychological tales of extrasensory perception and the occult. This development follows a trend in international children's fantasy exemplified by the stories of extrasensory perception, witchcraft, and demonic possession by the New Zealander Margaret Mahy.

One of the best fantasy-mysteries prior to 1975 is Janet Lunn's ghost story, *Double Spell* (1968). Much less childlike is Donn Kushner's curious and sophisticated ghost story, *Uncle Jacob's Ghost Story* (1984), which seems to blend the spirit of Isaac Bashevis Singer's realistic yet ghost-and-demon-populated stories of turn-of-the-century Jewish life in Polish ghettoes and New York City with a poetic magic realism similar to that of South American writers. This ghost story, which is also a love story, is framed by a grandfather's recitation to his grandson of the family legend of Uncle Jacob. It follows Jacob from a Polish ghetto to his news-stand on Times Square, where he is haunted by the ghosts of the two friends he loved most in life. The ghosts act out their dreams of being actors, singers, and dancers on the streets of New York under the tutelage of Mr Spangler, a bizarre, comic theatrical agent who is also the angel of death. The pathos, surrealism, and quirky humour give the narrative an adult sensibility and tone.

Such a tone is also found in Ruth Nichols's mature *Song of the Pearl* (1976). Although this narrative is framed by a ghostly apparition and visitation, it is not really a ghost story, but a philosophical investigation of life after death and of reincarnation. Nichols has an inventive imagination, supple enough to envision a credible, quasi-Bhuddist afterlife. The author's strong, clear writing is suited to her theme of power and the many shapes it takes: inner spiritual power, the power to manipulate other human beings, and the power to choose forgiveness over vengeance and hatred. Nichols explores the karmic patterns of sin, guilt, and redemption in the many incarnations of Mary Redmond, a twentieth-century teenager who undertakes a spiritual pilgrimage into her past lives, which include those of an Iroquois slave and a Sumerian king. The result is a sombre, densely textured, but very slow narrative, rich in literary and religious allusions.

By contrast, Welwyn Wilton Katz's *Witchery Hill* (1984), another tale of power and manipulation, moves at a breathless pace. The story concerns a contemporary Canadian boy who, while holidaying on the Channel Island of Guernsey, stumbles upon a murderous coven of witches. Though the book is a page-turner, it is unfortunately tainted by gratuitous, sensational violence.

Joan Clark, in *Wild Man of the Woods* (1985), also evokes the violence and terror associated with witchcraft and demonic possession. But her story is resonant with psychological overtones and strengthened by mythic patterns. And, through delicate foreshadowing, there is a satisfying inevitability and moral balance to the narrative when the mounting tension erupts in a violent, explosive climax. Like *Scarecrows* (1981), by the British author Robert Westall, this book combines the novel of character with the psychological thriller. The force of the protagonist's raw, ambivalent emotions of hate, fear, and self-distrust appear to cause destructive psychic activities in the real, physical world. This psychological shadow is not interpreted simplistically as externalized witchcraft, but as innate, a part of the continual struggle between good and evil in the human soul.

A shy Calgary boy, Stephen, travels to visit his relatives in the Rocky Mountain wilderness. His excitement at the beauty and magic of the landscape is heightened by his fascination with an old Indian mask carver, a giant of a man who lives alone in the forest, surrounded by his mysterious, totemistic masks. Cruel bullying by other children traumatizes Stephen until his own rage is released when he tries on the Indian mask of the Bookwas—the mythic cannibal wild man of the woods. The ferocious, devouring power of the myth and the mask possesses the boy, resulting in near-tragedy. The writing is vivid and forceful, but the book's special strength lies in its juxtaposition of surface realism with the mythic reality of a living, psychically charged Indian spirit world.

Christie Harris's fantasy and science-fiction works, such as *Secret in the Stlalakum Wild* (1972) and *Sky Man on the Totem Pole?* (1975), also attempt to depict the spiritual reality of the Indian world-view and to evoke the eerie power of the Canadian wilderness. But Clark's work is more coherent and disciplined. The believable characters and the authenticity of the boys' relationships balance the increasingly suspenseful, evocative atmosphere conveyed by the figurative language: metaphorical clusters composed of images of dark and light, of faces and masks, highlight the themes of the hidden, unknown self, of secret truths, of revelation and identity.

Perhaps the most powerful work in this category of the supernatural is also the most realistic. Cora Taylor's *Julie* (1985), like *Wild Man of the Woods*, speaks with the voice of surface realism, depicting an ordinary world populated by well-rounded characters living in a lovingly drawn prairie environment. The sense of 'otherness' in *Julie* lies in the psychic gift of the child protagonist, whose growing extra-sensory perception brings her alienation and grief. Taylor's prose, which is condensed and imagistic, has a richness of implication and mood that recall the elliptical style of the British author William Mayne.

The time span of this narrative, which follows the changeling-like Julie from ages three to ten, is unusual in a children's book, particularly because so much of the plot centres on Julie as a pre-schooler. Julie's Celtic second sight and psychic powers unfold in uncanny strength over the years, producing an alienating effect on others, including her mother. The omniscient narrative, which enables the reader to experience the mother's point of view, lends maturity and depth to the story. The final climax, in which Julie saves her father's life, is moving—though overburdened with a weight of incident and melodrama too heavy for the preceding delicacy of tone—but on the whole, the work succeeds in portraying with quiet drama an unusual child's perceptions and emotions.

Science Fiction

It would seem that science fiction appeals to the Canadian imagination more than other forms of fantasy. After all, such Canadian themes as the struggle for survival and its pragmatic considerations and the adaptation to new, hostile environments are also familiar motifs in the sociological, speculative, futuristic narratives of modern science fiction. Canadian science fiction written for children, however, is extremely rare. Canada has only one writer of international calibre, the remarkable Monica Hughes. Her work covers a broad age range, from light adventure-escapades for the intermediate reader to complex philosophical speculations for the young adult. Hughes's prolific output runs the gamut of science-fiction narratives, from those set on other planets to futuristic tales of life on earth after a nuclear, social, or economic disaster.

A major trend in international children's science fiction is a cosmopolitan outlook. But Hughes's writing, however global or universal her issues and themes, is informed by the Canadian immigrant and pioneer experience chronicled by Northrop Frye and Margaret Atwood. Hughes writes of space settlers, disoriented and adapting to a new and hostile planet, and of earth survivors struggling on a deteriorating planet; but regardless of the locale, the stories reflect the Canadian experience of being a lonely outsider, a stranger to a land that is too primal and vast to admit a human presence. Hughes explores ethical and moral dilemmas in the context of gripping adventures; whether the setting is earth, under the sea, the moon, or another planet, as in the *Isis* trilogy, her characters contend with psychological alienation and with survival while searching for human community in a threatening landscape.

The *Isis* trilogy is composed of *The Keeper of the Isis Light* (1980), *The Guardian of Isis* (1981), and *The Isis Pedlar* (1982). Set on the interstellar lighthouse planet of Isis in the twenty-first and twenty-second centuries, the trilogy follows the history of a community over four generations from its promising beginnings to near-destruction. Teen-aged Olwen has lived in isolation on the beautiful, alien planet of Isis with Guardian, her robot protector, since her earth parents' death. She has been physically altered by Guardian in order to acclimatize her to the harsh planet, and because of her inhuman, reptilian appearance the new group of Earth settlers spurns her. The existential dilemma of the outsider and such moral issues as prejudice and hatred are further extended in the sequels, in which the new settlement's president creates a totalitarian dystopia, a society that rewrites its history as superstition and taboo.

Though Hughes's stories are certainly within the science-fiction category of the 'writing of ideas'—the speculative literature devoted to 'what if?' questions—they are not clinically abstract. The scientific detail is tightly controlled; the style is direct and economical; the plots have a subtle momentum that extends their scope beyond that of the powerful but predictable and mechanical futuristic action-dramas of Douglas Hill (*The Huntsman*, 1982) and Martin Godfrey (*The Vandarian Incident*, 1981). Moving relationships among rounded, indomitable characters add dramatic tension and narrative depth to Hughes's plots. A memorable character is the robot, Guardian, whose devotion to Olwen bridges the gulf between the alien and the human and poses one of Hughes's recurring questions: what does it mean to be human?

One preoccupation in Hughes's work is the role of technology. This is often expressed in the conflict between the new scientific knowledge that may save or destroy the planet and the old, traditional knowledge, especially the native peoples' wisdom, which entails respect for, and survival on, the earth. Both *Ring-Rise, Ring-Set* (1982) and *Beyond the Dark River* (1979), two parallel works set in a future Canada after natural and social disasters, reveal Hughes's fascination with the infinite variety of human societies and the ways in which different communities relate to the earth and to women.

In *Ring-Rise, Ring-Set*, the imminent disaster of a new Ice Age threatens the earth. A colony of scientists living in an underground city in the Canadian North is desperately searching for a solution—and destroying the ecology of the land through their experiments. Life in an isolated, dystopian society—subterranean or enclosed, but symbolically alienated from the natural world—is also examined in other post-disaster novels: Suzanne Martel's simpler *The City Under Ground* (1964) and Hughes's own *Devil on My Back* (1985). In all these works a teen-aged protagonist breaks free from the stifling city to explore the outside world. After venturing forth from her enclosed city and becoming lost in the ice fields, Liza, in *Ring-Rise, Ring-Set*, is rescued by a nomadic tribe of Ekoes (a portmanteau name combining ecology and eskimo). Psychologically, Liza takes on the identity of a dead Ekoe girl and forms a bond with the more emotionally nurturing, ecologically rooted people.

The communication difficulties between ethnocentric groups, complicated by the psychological differences in human thought, which depends on cultural belief systems, is also a theme of *Beyond the Dark River*. A post-disaster narrative set in the vicinity of Edmonton in the twenty-first century after what appears to be a nuclear catastrophe, it relates the moving friendship between teenagers from the two cultures who are self-sufficient enough to survive the disaster. A Cree-Indian girl who is her tribe's Healer joins a Hutterite youth on his search for medical aid to help his settlement's dying children. The journey by river into destroyed Edmonton, the City of the Dead, has mythic overtones, recalling the night sea-journey into the unknown and the unconscious. The quest becomes a terrifying rite of passage as the young people learn to value each other's complex heritage, spirit, and disparate personalities, and to unite their strengths for survival.

Of all the writing for children that explores Canada's multiculturalism, Hughes's science fiction is the most thought-provoking. She dramatizes the meeting of cultures and makes vividly concrete the invaluable, living heritage of a society's myth, ritual, and history. Her writing is not only a plea for tolerance and respect among ethnic groups, but a summons to survival—the survival of a rich panoply of cultures in Canada, and, by implication, on the earth. And finally, by the urgent force of Hughes's conviction, her science fiction calls for global survival.

In the decade from 1975 to 1985 Canadian fiction for children and young adults experienced an imaginative midwifery and a vigorous growth. Although not fully mature, it is developing a scope and a depth that hold promise for the future. A substantial portion of the new literature is Canadian in content or context, but little of it is ethnocentric. A coherent sense of identity is emerging from the literature, however, whether the story-tellers describe the experience of 'home' in the narrative cadences of everyday realistic life, or whether they explore further afield in historical or fantastical intonations. Like the Canadian pioneer so dominant in our cultural imagination, the best of our story-tellers are blazing trails for those who follow.

ALDERSON, SUE ANN. *The Not Impossible Summer*. Illustrations by Christina Rother. Toronto, Clarke, 1983, paper.

BELLINGHAM, BRENDA. *Storm Child*. Toronto, Lorimer, 1985, cloth, paper (Time of Our Lives)

BRADFORD, KARLEEN. *The Other Elizabeth*. Illustrations by Deborah Drew-Brook. Toronto, Gage, 1982, paper, educ. edn (Jeanpac Books)

BRANDIS, MARIANNE. *The Quarter-Pie Window*. With original wood engravings by G. Brender à Brandis. Erin, Ont., Porcupine's Quill, 1985, paper.

_____. *The Tinder Box: A Novel*. With original wood engravings by G. Brender à Brandis. Erin, Ont., Porcupine's Quill, 1982, cloth (O.P.), paper.

BROCHMANN, ELIZABETH. *Nobody Asked Me*. Toronto, Lorimer, 1984, cloth, paper (Time of our Lives)

CLARK, JOAN. *The Hand of Robin Squires*. Illustrations by William Taylor and Mary Cserepy. Toronto/Vancouver, Clarke, 1977, cloth (O.P.); 1981, paper, educ. edn; Markham, Ont., Penguin, 1986, paper.

_____. *Wild Man of the Woods*. Markham, Ont., Viking, 1985, cloth; Markham, Ont., Penguin, 1986, paper.

COLLURA, MARY-ELLEN LANG. *Winners*. Saskatoon, Sask., Western, 1984, paper.

CRAIG, JOHN. *Chappie and Me*. New York, Dodd, 1979, cloth (O.P.); Reprinted under title: *Ain't Lookin'*. Richmond Hill, Ont., Scholastic-TAB, 1983, paper.

CULLETON, BEATRICE. *In Search of April Raintree*. Winnipeg, Pemmican, 1983, paper (O.P.); Rev. edn under title: *April Raintree*, 1984, paper.

DOYLE, BRIAN. *Angel Square*. Vancouver/Toronto, Douglas, 1984, paper (A Groundwood Book)

_____. *Hey, Dad!* Toronto, Groundwood, 1978, cloth (O.P.), paper.

_____. *Up to Low*. Vancouver, Douglas, 1982, paper (A Groundwood Book)

_____. *You Can Pick Me Up at Peggy's Cove*. Illustrated by Heather Collins. Toronto, Groundwood, 1979, cloth (O.P.), paper.

DUNCAN, FRANCES. *Kap-Sung Ferris*. Toronto, Burns, 1977, paper; Toronto, Macmillan, 1982, paper.

FREEMAN, BILL. *Harbour Thieves*. Toronto, Lorimer, 1984, cloth, paper (Adventures in Canadian History)

FRYER, MARY BEACOCK. *Escape: Adventures of a Loyalist Family*. Illustrations by Stephen Clarke. Don Mills, Ont., Dent, 1976, paper (O.P.); Toronto/Charlottetown, Dundurn, 1982, paper.

GERMAN, TONY. *Tom Penny*. Illustrated by Diana McElroy. Toronto, Martin, 1977, cloth (O.P.), paper (O.P.); Toronto, M & S, 1983, paper.

GODFREY, MARTYN. *The Vandarian Incident*. Richmond Hill, Ont., Scholastic-TAB, 1981, paper.

GREENWOOD, BARBARA. *A Question of Loyalty*. Richmond Hill, Ont., Scholastic-TAB, 1984, paper.

HALVORSON, MARILYN. *Cowboys Don't Cry*. Toronto, Clarke, 1984, paper.

_____. *Let It Go*. Toronto, Irwin, 1985, paper.

HARRIS, CHRISTIE. *Secret in the Stlalakum Wild*. Illustrated by Douglas Tait. Toronto/Montreal, M & S, 1972, cloth (O.P.)

_____. *Sky Man on the Totem Pole?* Illustrated by Douglas Tait. Toronto, M & S, 1975, cloth.

HEWITT, MARSHA AND CLAIRE MACKAY. *One Proud Summer*. Toronto, Women's Press, 1981, paper.

HILL, DOUGLAS. *The Huntsman*. London/Toronto, Heinemann, 1982, cloth (O.P.)

HOUSTON, JAMES. *Black Diamonds: A Search for Arctic Treasure*. Drawings by the author. Toronto, M & S, 1982, cloth; Markham, Ont., Puffin, 1983, paper.

_____. *Frozen Fire: A Tale of Courage*. Drawings by the author. Toronto, M & S, 1977, cloth (O.P.); Markham, Ont., Puffin, 1979, paper.

_____. *Ice Swords: An Undersea Adventure*. Drawings by the author. Toronto, M & S, 1985, cloth.

_____. *Long Claws: An Arctic Adventure*. Illustrated by the author. Toronto, M & S, 1981, cloth.

_____. *River Runners: A Tale of Hardship and Bravery*. Drawings by the author. Toronto, M & S, 1979, cloth (O.P.); Markham, Ont., Penguin, 1981, paper.

HUDSON, JAN. *Sweetgrass*. Edmonton, Tree Frog, 1984, paper.

HUGHES, MONICA. *Beyond the Dark River*. Don Mills, Ont., Nelson, 1979, cloth (O.P.)

_____. *Devil on My Back*. London, MacRae, 1984, cloth.

_____. *The Guardian of Isis*. Toronto, Clarke, 1981, cloth (O.P.)

_____. *Hunter in the Dark*. Toronto/Vancouver, Clarke, 1982, cloth; Toronto, Avon, 1984, paper.

_____. *The Isis Pedlar*. Scarborough, Ont., Fleet, 1982, cloth (O.P.)

_____. *The Keeper of the Isis Light*. Toronto, Nelson, 1980, cloth (O.P.)

_____. *My Name is Paula Popowich!* Illustrated by Leoung O'Young. Toronto, Lorimer, 1983, cloth, paper (Time of Our Lives)

_____. *Ring-Rise, Ring-Set*. Toronto, Watts, 1982, cloth (O.P.)

HUNTER, BERNICE THURMAN. *As Ever, Booky*. Richmond Hill, Ont., Scholastic-TAB, 1985, paper.

_____. *That Scatterbrain Booky*. Richmond Hill, Ont., Scholastic-TAB, 1981, paper.

_____. *With Love from Booky*. Richmond Hill, Ont., Scholastic-TAB, 1983, paper.

KATZ, WELWYN WILTON. *Witchery Hill*. Vancouver/Toronto, Douglas, 1984, paper (A Groundwood Book)

KELLERHALS-STEWART, HEATHER. *Stuck Fast in Yesterday*. Vancouver/Toronto, Douglas, 1983, paper (A Groundwood Book)

KORMAN, GORDON. *Don't Care High*. New York, Scholastic, 1985, cloth (O.P.); 1986, paper.

_____. *This Can't Be Happening at Macdonald Hall!* Richmond Hill, Ont., Scholastic-TAB, 1978, paper; Rev. edn, 1980, paper (Bruno and Boots).

KUSHNER, DONN. *Uncle Jacob's Ghost Story*. Toronto, Macmillan, 1984, cloth.

_____. *The Violin-Maker's Gift*. Illustrated by Doug Panton. Toronto, Macmillan, 1980, cloth.

LAURENCE, MARGARET. *The Olden Days Coat*. Illustrated by Muriel Wood. Toronto, M & S, 1979, paper (O.P.); Rev. edn, 1982, cloth.

LITTLE, JEAN. *From Anna*. Pictures by Joan Sandin. Toronto, Fitzhenry, 1972, cloth (O.P.); 2nd edn, 1977, paper (The Contemporary Scene)

_____. *Listen for the Singing*. Toronto, Clarke, 1977, cloth (O.P.); 1981, paper.

_____. *Lost and Found*. Illustrated by Leoung O'Young. Markham, Ont., Viking, 1985, cloth; Markham, Ont., Penguin, 1986, paper.

_____. *Mama's Going to Buy You a Mockingbird*. Markham, Ont., Viking, 1984, cloth; Markham, Ont., Puffin, 1985, paper.

LUNN, JANET. *Double Spell*. Illustrated by A.M. Calder. Toronto, Martin, 1968, cloth (O.P.); Toronto, Clarke, 1983, paper; Markham, Ont., Penguin, 1986, paper (Title of American edition: *Twin Spell*)

_____. *The Root Cellar*. Toronto, Lester and Orpen, 1981, cloth (O.P.), paper; Markham, Ont., Puffin, 1983, paper.

MACKAY, CLAIRE. *The Minerva Program*. Toronto, Lorimer, 1984, cloth, paper (Time of Our Lives)

McKEEVER, KATHERINE. *Granny's Gang: Life with a Most Unusual Family of Owls*. Illustrated by Olena Kassian. Toronto, Greey de Pencier, 1984, paper (An OWL Magazine Book)

McNEIL, FLORENCE. *All Kinds of Magic*. Vancouver/Toronto, Douglas, 1984, paper (A Groundwood Book)

_____. *Miss P. and Me*. Toronto/Vancouver, Clarke, 1982, cloth; Richmond Hill, Ont., Scholastic-TAB, 1984, paper.

MAILLET, ANTONINE. *Christopher Cartier of Hazelnut, Also Known as Bear*. Translated by Wayne Grady. Toronto, Methuen, 1984, cloth (First published in French, 1981)

MAJOR, KEVIN. *Far from Shore*. Toronto, Clarke, 1980, cloth (O.P.)

_____. *Hold Fast*. Toronto/Vancouver, Clarke, 1978, cloth (O.P.), paper.

_____. *Thirty-six Exposures*. Toronto, Doubleday, 1984, cloth.

MARKOOSIE. *Harpoon of the Hunter*. Illustrations by Germaine Arnaktauyok. Montreal/London, McGill-Queen's, 1970, cloth, paper.

MARTEL, SUZANNE. *The City Under Ground*. Translated by Norah Smaridge. Toronto/Vancouver, Douglas, 1982, paper (A Groundwood Book) (First published in French, 1966)

_____. *The King's Daughter*. Translated by David Toby Homel and Margaret Rose. Illustrations by Debi Perna. Vancouver, Douglas, 1980, cloth, paper (A Groundwood Book) (First published in French, 1974).

MELLING, O.R.. *The Druid's Tune*. Markham, Ont., Kestrel, 1983, cloth, paper; Markham, Ont., Penguin, 1984, paper.

MONTERO, GLORIA. *The Summer the Whales Sang*. Toronto, Lorimer, 1985, cloth, paper (Time of Our Lives)

MOWAT, FARLEY M. *Owls in the Family*. Illustrated by Robert Frankenberg. Boston/Toronto, Little, 1961, cloth (O.P.); Toronto, M & S, 1973, paper; M & S, 1980, collector's edn.

NICHOLS, RUTH. *The Left-Handed Spirit*. Toronto, Macmillan, 1978, cloth (O.P.)

_____. *Song of the Pearl*. Toronto, Macmillan, 1976, cloth (O.P.)

PAPERNY, MYRA. *The Wooden People*. Illustrated by Ken Stampnick. Boston/Toronto, Little, 1976, cloth (O.P.)

PASNAK, WILLIAM. *In the City of the King*. Vancouver/Toronto, Douglas, 1984, paper (A Groundwood Book)

PATTERSON, NANCY-LOU. *Apple Staff and Silver Crown: A Fairy Tale*. Erin, Ont., Porcupine's Quill, 1985, paper.

RAZZELL, MARY. *Snow Apples*. Vancouver/Toronto, Douglas, 1984, paper (A Groundwood Book)

RICHLER, MORDECAI. *Jacob Two-Two Meets the Hooded Fang*. Illustrated by Fritz Wegner. Toronto, M & S, 1975, cloth; Toronto, Seal, 1981, paper.

RICHMOND, SANDRA. *Wheels for Walking*. Vancouver/Toronto, Douglas, 1983, paper (A Groundwood Book)

ROY, GABRIELLE. *Cliptail*. Translated by Alan Brown. Illustrated by François Olivier. Toronto, M & S, 1980, paper (First published in French, 1979)

SASS, GREGORY. *Redcoat*. Erin, Ont., Porcupine's Quill, 1985, paper.

SMUCKER, BARBARA CLAASSEN. *Amish Adventure*. Toronto/Vancouver, Clarke, 1983, paper; Markham, Ont., Puffin, 1984, paper.

_____. *Days of Terror*. Toronto/Vancouver, Clarke, 1979, cloth; Markham, Ont., Puffin, 1981, paper.

_____. *Underground to Canada*. Toronto/Vancouver, Clarke, 1977, cloth; Markham, Ont., Puffin, 1978, paper.

_____. *White Mist*. Toronto, Irwin, 1985, paper.

STREN, PATTI. *I Was a 15-Year-Old Blimp*. Toronto, Irwin, 1985, cloth.

_____. *There's a Rainbow in My Closet*. Illustrated by the author. Toronto, Fitzhenry, 1979, cloth (O.P.)

TAYLOR, CORA. *Julie*. Saskatoon, Sask., Western, 1985, paper.

TENNANT, VERONICA. *On Stage, Please: A Story*. Illustrations by Rita Briansky. Toronto, M & S, 1977, cloth (O.P.); Rev. edn, paper.

TRUSS, JAN. *Jasmin*. Vancouver, Douglas, 1982, paper (A Groundwood Book)

WALSH, ANN. *Your Time, My Time*. Victoria/Toronto, Porcépic, 1984, cloth (O.P.), paper.

WATERTON, BETTY. *Quincy Rumpel*. Vancouver/Toronto, Douglas, 1984, paper (A Groundwood Book)

YEE, PAUL. *Teach Me to Fly, Skyfighter! and Other Stories*. Illustrated by Sky Lee. Toronto, Lorimer, 1983, cloth, paper (The Adventure in Canada Series)

4

THE ORAL TRADITION

The family tree of children's literature with its many branches of picture-books, fiction, folklore, mythology, legend, and poetry, has its roots in the rich soil of the oral tradition. From infancy, children are introduced to song, story, and rhyme through the spoken voice of a loving adult, as each generation passes on to the next the heritage of human memory and literary lore. This legacy, preserved by oral transmission, encompasses a wide range of literary forms. Children's first poetry is the oral literature of song and chant, lullaby and nursery rhyme. Picture-books are generally intended to be read aloud by adult to child. Children's own subculture lore of street and game rhymes constitutes an oral folk poetry. Poetry written for children comes alive when it is chanted in groups or recited aloud. And, of course, the ancient and anonymous narratives of folktale, myth, and legend, as old as language itself, are the staples of oral story-telling, having persisted in human memory over centuries. The literary art and psychological depth of these narratives form the very ground of children's literature, deeply influencing the content and structure of fiction for children.

In Canada the tradition of folklore, mythology, and legend has flourished in oral accounts and tales drawn from the culture and history of the four major components of our population: the aboriginal peoples (native Indian and Inuit), the French-Canadians and Anglo-Canadians, and the other ethnic groups of the multicultural mosaic.

Separately, these bodies of folklore reflect the ethnic values and history of each distinct group and form the cultural heritage of a people. Taken together, these diverse traditions tentatively shape developing patterns of a new national lore, which gives voice to the Canadian aboriginal and immigrant experience and embodies the landscape, while echoing the universal, archetypal themes of international folklore.

ABORIGINAL FOLKLORE, MYTHOLOGY, AND LEGEND

Beginning with the first non-anthropological collection, Pauline Johnson's *Legends of Vancouver* (1911), the oral tales of the aboriginal peoples have been collected and written down for a non-native audience in many different styles throughout this century. Although originally created as oral lore for native adults and children, the interpretation and shaping of this material for contemporary children has been surrounded by controversy and debate. In addition to the difficulties of translating and transcribing an art form based on oral transmission into a new written shape, there are specific problems associated with retellings for children. These include the question of who should tell the stories (how valid are non-native retellings of native lore?); how the story should be told in order to balance research and scholarship with authenticity and literary shaping; how to avoid stereotypes; and how to provide a context that retains narrative values and a flavour of place and custom. To make these stories understandable to non-native children, it may be necessary to shape the original multiform and loosely structured native lore into western story patterns. But an expurgation of the violence, sexuality, and scatology inherent in the tales, or a contemporary revision that alters so-called images of sexism, can produce a sanitization that invariably distorts the original meaning.

Despite these difficulties for the adult reteller, children have always exhibited a strong appetite for the stories of the oral tradition, and creators of Canadian children's literature have responded with retellings of native folklore, mythology, and legend. Often these are the stories that answered the questions of preliterate societies: myth as a metaphorical explanation of customs, traditions, and natural phenomena; and legend as a poetic drama with a kernel of historical truth. But, more importantly, these stories also embody the most significant social and psychological values of their culture. The work of Canadian retellers of native lore since the 1960s has been recognized both nationally and internationally as a major strength in Canadian children's literature.

Indian Folklore, Mythology, and Legend

Canadian native Indian lore, with its nature stories, myths of creation and culture heroes, and archetypal images of world flood or theft of light and fire, is uniquely dramatic and mysterious. Early retellings, such as Cyrus Macmillan's romantic *Canadian Wonder Tales* (1918), gave way to the more scholarly and authentic interpretations of the 1960s, such as Christie Harris's *Once Upon a Totem* (1963), as well as to the reclaiming and preserving of legends by native retellers, as in George Clutesi's *Son of Raven, Son of Deer: Fables of the Tse-Shaht People* (1967). The late 1960s also saw an international trend towards publishing picture-book editions of single illustrated folktales, exemplified in Canada by the illustrated Indian legends produced by Elizabeth Cleaver and William Toye. A parallel interest in the oral ritual poetry found in aboriginal song and chant was evident in the early 1970s with the appearance of collections such as James Houston's *Songs of the Dream People: Chants and Images from the Indians and Eskimos of North America* (1972).

Along with society's increased sensitivity to the rights of minority groups and the growing cultural life of the indigenous peoples of Canada since the early 1970s came an increase in programs of Native Studies and publications of native lore. Collections for children now reflect the entire geographic and linguistic breadth of Canada, from the Kwaikiutl, Haida, and Tlingit tribes of the Pacific Northwest Coast chronicled by Christie Harris to the Nova Scotian tribal lore retold by Alden Nowlan in *Nine Micmac Legends* (1983).

Foremost among the non-native retellers is Christie Harris, whose intimate knowledge of British Columbia's mountains, forests and seascape, empathy for the Indian world-view, and well researched ethnological source material give authenticity and cultural context to her collections. Harris's experience as a radio scriptwriter has enabled her to write for the ear as well as for the printed page; her retellings possess elements of the oral story-teller's voice, such as recurring verbal patterns and sentence fragments. Harris embellishes the often bald style of the originals, emphasizing their mystical atmosphere and deepening characterization.

In her recent *Mouse Woman* trilogy, illustrated by Douglas Tait (*Mouse Woman and the Mischief-Makers*, 1977; *Mouse Woman and the Muddleheads*, 1979; *Mouse Woman and the Vanished Princesses*, 1976), Harris lightens her approach, introducing humour and intimacy through the character of Mouse Woman, a narnauk or shape-shifting spirit-guide. Mouse Woman acts as an endearing link between legends; in story-cycles on the themes of balance, order, and justice in the universe, this tiny being—half-grandmother, half-mouse—helps restore harmony to the lives of young people. These moral themes continue in Harris's companion volumes: *The Trouble with Princesses* (1980) and *The Trouble with Adventurers* (1982). Both sequences of books are intriguing attempts to give a structure to the amorphous shape of native lore. In the *Mouse Woman* trilogy, the recurring character of the narnauk provides continuity; in *The Trouble with Princesses*, short introductions connect the spirited Indian princesses with those of European folklore. The strong coming-of-age themes in these stories of adolescent crises thrust the princesses into rights-of-passage adventures with gently erotic undertones.

Like Harris's retellings, Joan Skogan's *Princess and the Sea-Bear and Other Tsimshian Stories* (1983), which was originally broadcast on the CBC, evokes the Northwest-coast landscape and, without bowdlerizing the original tales, gives a sense of dramatic conflict and romance to their primal violence and sexuality.

Cycles of legends gain unity not only through modest, cosy figures like the busybody Mouse Woman but through larger, more mythic central characters—culture-heroes and trickster-gods, such as Nana-bozho and Raven. The psychological and moral complexity of these half-animal, half-human figures, the sly humour and epic drama of their adventures, make rich and fertile legends. Several collections focus on Raven, Robert Ayre's early quest-cycle *Sketco the Raven* (1961) and Gail Robinson's less successful *Raven the Trickster: Legends of the North American Indians* (1981) are story-cycles that attempt to portray the foolish, greedy, cruel, and beneficent trickster figure. Quite different from this traditional structure of separate tales is the single narrative, *Raven's Children: A Novel Based on the Myths of the*

Northwest Coast Indians (1979), by Yves Troendle. This saga of a heroic journey by a brother and sister through the societies of the Northwest uses the myths as strong metaphors and images, much as the native American Indian novelist Jamake Highwater does in his epic novels based on Indian legend. Despite the unevenness of many of these reworkings, they are truer to the deeply human, all-encompassing, and erratic spirit of Raven than Anne Cameron's feminist, revisionist version, *How Raven Freed the Moon* (1985), which arbitrarily changes the traditionally male figure of Raven to a female persona.

By contrast, the image of Raven portrayed in legends re-created by native retellers is truer and, at times, the material remains unadulterated and raw. George Clutesi's early *Son of Raven, Son of Deer* is a collection of humorous fables that entertain and instruct. Raven is an animal-fable trickster; his mild and amusing escapades are told in easy, colloquial diction that is touched by poetry and warm humour, and conveys a completely natural sense of belief.

A harsher, more provocative, and poignant collection of Raven myths is the meticulous recasting of the legends for an adult audience by native artist Bill Reid and poet Robert Bringhurst. *The Raven Steals the Light* (1984) contains the lyricism, sexuality, scatology, trickery, and polymorphous dream-potency of the original legends, although the bawdy elements are somewhat tempered by Reid's fine pencil drawings and by the elegiac, bittersweet tone of the narrator's voice in asides that lament the passing traditions of a lost native heritage. Like the blind Homeric storyteller in Leon Garfield and Edward Blishen's Greek myth cycle, *The Golden Shadow* (1973), Reid and Bringhurst's narrator speaks as one who heard the legends with total belief as a child and now experiences their diminishing power as an adult.

Métis writer Maria Campbell, in *Little Badger and the Fire Spirit* (1977), evokes in a contrasting fashion the native child's point of view and is more optimistic about cultural continuity. Campbell's picture-storybook is an archetypal fire-quest legend framed by a contemporary native-family story. An Alberta Indian girl leaves the city to visit her grandparents, who live in a log house and follow the old traditional hunting and trapping ways; they tell her the fire legend that lives in their personal and tribal memories. Here, the sense of elegiac loss portrayed in *The Raven Steals the Light* is transformed into an awareness of a living oral tradition, in which the time of the myth is not distant, but vigorously present: it survives across time and generations through the power of story-telling. Campbell's blend of realism and legend emphasizes the continuity of the mythic hero-quest and its presence in contemporary native life.

Other publications created by native retellers include single picture-book legends for both native and non-native children. Small, commercial native publishers, from Pemmican Publications to Theytus Books, and native cultural groups, such as the Okanagan Tribal Council, recast and illustrate legends, often from the taped, colloquial story-telling of tribal elders, such as that found in Murdo Scribe's animal fable *Murdo's Story: A Legend from Northern Manitoba* (1985).

Sometimes the native reteller may use a more formal, less idiomatic style, as in Basil Johnston's *Tales the Elders Told: Ojibway Legends* (1981). A native Ojibway and ethnologist at the Royal Ontario Museum, Johnston retells stories he collected from Ojibway elders. His style is simpler and more direct than the subtle, poetic diction of Reid and Bringhurst, but his short sentences are choppy and rough compared to the natural flow of words in a parallel collection, *The Adventures of Nanabush: Ojibway Indian Stories* (1979). Recorded and compiled by Emerson and David Coatsworth from legends told by Rama Ojibway Band elders, this collection reworks the inflections of various elders into a confiding voice that seems to belong to a single contemporary story-teller. In asides and introductions, the narrator looks back to the early days of the creation myths and 'pourquoi' stories and to the old Ojibway story-tellers who shared a cosmological vision and a belief in the spiritual truth of the legends. The native Eastern Woodland-style paintings by Francis Kagige are as emotionally convincing as the deft native retellings.

Inuit Folklore, Mythology, and Legend

Retellings of Inuit myth and legend for children were slower to develop and remain fewer in number than those from the Indian tradition. And the earthiness, seemingly rambling, fragmentary structure, and harsh world-view of Inuit tales present even more problems to the reteller for children. Non-Inuit writers, whose versions attained a middle-ground of modified and coherent composition while avoiding bowd-lerization and excessive modern embellishments, include James Houston and Ronald Melzack. Their work in the late 1960s and early 1970s—such as Houston's Inuit legend picture-book, *Kiviok's Magic Journey: An Eskimo Legend* (1973)—created heroic legends and sim-ple folk-narratives from a complex mass of undifferentiated lore. Their retellings evoked the very real Inuit spirit-world and the power of shamanism, the harsh and beautiful northern landscape, and the strict social laws and human codes of courage and stoicism.

Since the mid-1970s there has been little recasting of Inuit lore for children. James Houston has concentrated on young-adult fiction of survival and heroism rather than on the native tales, while Ronald Melzack, in his *Why the Man in the Moon is Happy and Other Eskimo Creation Stories* (1977), continues his approach of softening these severe and complex tales to an accessible but, at times, simplistic level. By contrast, Garnet Hewitt's picture-storybook, *Ytek and the Arctic Orchid* (1981)—a classic story of shamanism and a rites-of-passage quest—is filled with complex psychological and archetypal meaning.

Retellings by native Inuit people of their folk materials have not been numerous. Before 1975 there were only a few collections of edited and translated tales transcribed from the tellings of Inuit elders, such as Maurice Metayer's *Tales from the Igloo* (1972). Like the first piece of fiction written by an Inuit—Markoosie's *Harpoon of the Hunter* (1970)—Metayer's work is true to the dream-like structure, the bleak stoicism, and the monstrous nightmare figures so integral to Inuit mythology. However, such elements are usually altered or expurgated for a non-native child audience.

Stories from Pangnirtung (1976), a companion volume to *Tales from the Igloo*, is more oral history than mythology. Composed of stories from Inuit survivors of the old nomadic life, these memoirs include folk elements of traditional customs and traditions.

Similar folk customs and fragments of myth and ritual are present in the collections of Inuit poetry: the songs, chants, and incantations that appear in Inuit narratives and accompany religious rituals and daily life. Before 1975 anthologies such as the American Richard Lewis's *I Breathe a New Song: Poems of the Eskimo* (1971) and James Houston's *Songs of the Dream People* were compiled for a dual child-and-adult audience. The freshness and simple diction of these traditional lyrics, their sharpness of image and music, and their celebration of the natural world are similar to qualities found in children's own writing. The anthologies published in the last decade, such as John Robert Colombo's *Poems of the Inuit* (1981), which contain powerful folk poetry and are accurately rendered from the transcriptions and translations of early cultural anthropologists, are too overburdened with scholarly apparatus to be suitable for a child audience.

FRENCH-CANADIAN FOLKLORE

Another rich body of Canadian folklore is found in French Canada: folk-and-wonder tales in the European tradition, remembered and retold from the French originals, and new indigenous lore and local legends, developed by the French-Canadian settlers. These include traditional wonder tales of Petit Jean, the youngest son, who appears in the folk-sagas; supernatural and religious tales of sorcerers and the Devil; and tales of saints, priests, and nuns, of flying witch-canoes and werewolves.

Since 1975 no collections of folklore have achieved the vitality and grace of Claude Aubry's adult *Magic Fiddler and Other Legends of French Canada* (1968) or the distinguished first book of non-native folktales for children, Marius Barbeau's *Golden Phoenix and Other French-Canadian Fairy Tales* (1958). Two anthologies published since 1975, Mary Alice Downie's *Witch of the North: Folk Tales of French Canada* (1975) and Edith Fowke's scholarly reference work for adults, *Folktales of French Canada* (1981), are both valuable resources. *The Witch of the North*, although designed for children, is adult in content and uneven in style, at times oddly flat, with little of the imaginative zest or careful shaping that would attract children. The collage illustrations by Elizabeth Cleaver are delicate but murky, conveying a sense of eerie foreboding that suits the macabre tone of many of the tales.

The adult sensibility and sophistication found in many of the satirical French-Canadian tales are also present in Michael Macklem's humorous, earthy *Jacques the Woodcutter* (1977). Originally a fabliau or comic story embellished with songs, it is reworked here and told with a curiously awkward pacing as a plain narrative picture-book farce of implied adultery and deception. The plot's lack of clarity is echoed in Ann Blades's illustrations, which are usually fine in her other works but here are vague and confusing.

By contrast, the picture-book *The Wicked Fairy-Wife: A French Canadian Folktale* (1983), with a polished text by Mary Alice Downie and illustrations by Kim Price, flows with narrative energy. A powerful European-style folktale of romantic love and violent revenge, its frightening details are true to the classic folk struggle between good and evil.

ANGLO-CANADIAN FOLKLORE

Anglo-Canadian folk materials are fragmentary and regional; there is no cohesive body of lore, nor is there a wealth of collected interpretations for children, such as those taken from French-Canadian and indigenous native legend. Most anthologies devoted to general Canadian folklore tend to rework a cross-section of Indian and Inuit tales and French and Anglo-Celtic Canadian lore. The result is a mixture of tales that reveal the transposition of folk roots and heritage: Old World lore is adapted to the New World, blended with the Canadian climate and landscape, and altered by the immigrant experience. Additional components are regional local legends, pioneer tall tales, yarns, anecdotes, and ghost stories composed in Canada. Such collections may be national or regional in focus. Examples include the scholarly, adult-oriented *Folklore of Canada* (1976) by Edith Fowke, and the less scholarly *Storytellers' Rendezvous: Canadian Stories to Tell to Children* (1979) and *Storytellers' Encore: More Canadian Stories To Tell to Children* (1984), compiled by Lorrie Andersen, Irene Aubrey, and Louise McDiarmid, both of which are anthologies designed for adult use as practical source-books for story-tellers.

The most important collection of this folk material designed for an actual child audience is Eva Martin's *Canadian Fairy Tales* (1984). As elegantly produced as Cyrus Macmillan's sumptuous early twentieth-century gift-books of Canadian lore, Martin's collection has a flamboyant richness of illustration and a curiously lean text that has been purged of the colour and pungency of local speech. The manner

of telling is so bone-bare that the stories seem to be cryptic conden-
sations of incidents; for completion they need the natural warmth,
colloquialism, amplification, and embellishment of the oral story-
teller's voice. No native lore is included, only the adapted stories of
settlers, transplanted from their English and French roots. These are
not overtly New World Tales. Most are classic folktales with a few
pioneer motifs and many elements of faerie, such as giants, princesses,
and witches. The familiar plots abound with marvellous enchantments,
quests, and the violent confict of good and evil. There are some
original touches, for example, the anomalous reversal of the original
in the Canadian version of 'Beauty and the Beast,' in which the
heroine changes from beast to princess.

Laszlo Gal's artwork metaphorically parallels the text. Black and
white line drawings, which provide decorative borders for the full-
colour paintings, suggest an artist-explorer's sketchbook of pioneer
life. Picturing the flora and fauna of a new land, and the ever-present
wilderness, the drawings are as laconic and bare as the prose, but,
unlike the unlocalized text, they convey a sense of the Canadian
setting that surrounds the timeless fairy tales. These lean, New World
images are a manifestation of the 'garrison mentality'. They not only
frame but subtly dominate the European-style colour illustrations,
which are set-pieces that recall the golden age of children's-book
illustration and the original, romantic fairy-tale tradition of the Old
World. In the Canadian versions of the folktales, the metaphorical
quests and adventures that take place in the symbolic, perilous wood
of European faerie become real struggles to find an actual path through
the dark and dangerous Canadian forest. The juxtaposition of the two
different art styles echoes the transformation of Old World folklore
into New World legend that lies at the heart of these stories. The
romantic, Old World wonder-tales are seen here, in both text and
illustration, as pared down to their core, reduced by the harsh Canadian
environment and pioneer 'garrison mentality', and absorbed into a
new lore that is a down-to-earth, survival-oriented variant of the old.

The impact of the New World landscape and wildlife on the mythopoeic folk imagination was evident even before the settlers' experience.
From the time of the Norsemen it can be seen in the written and oral
accounts of the first explorers, traders, adventurers, and missionaries
who came to North America. Mary Hamilton's *New World Bestiary*

(1985) is a fascinating selection from these early travel writings and reports that blends memoir and historical fact into fabulous new legend, forming a parallel to the medieval mythic bestiaries. These fragmentary impressions and tales of New-World creatures and monsters of the imagination, such as the Sasquatch of British Columbia and the St Lawrence cannibal Gou-Gou, interpret new experience through the archetypes of the unconscious. Kim La Fave's powerful drawings in rough red conté and paintings in full colour have a dark, shadowy atmosphere of mystery. They reflect the fear and excitement inspired by these mythic images—imaginary marvels discovered in the travellers' voyages into the unknown and the unconscious.

In a lighter vein, a trio of picture-books demonstrates the emergence in Canada of a local, indigenous folklore with a regional perspective and flavour: Carole Spray's pioneer noodlehead tale, *The Mare's Egg: A New World Folk Tale* (1981); Joan Finnigan's Ottawa Valley logging-camp tall-tale, *Look! The Land is Growing Giants: A Very Canadian Legend* (1983); and Jenni Lunn's contemporary, revisionist, Nova-Scotian treatment of the Grimm tale, *The Fisherman and His Wife* (1982). Both linguistically and emotionally, all three possess a particularly Canadian diction and idiom.

In *The Mare's Egg*, the teasing of the gullible greenhorn—a genteel immigrant tricked by the working-class pioneers into believing that a pumpkin would hatch a foal—is a familiar device. Folktales about fools are widespread, and this event could take place anywhere in pioneer North America, but the reserve and restraint of the tricksters and the sly, ironic humour in Spray's text and in Kim La Fave's Maritime illustrations link the story to T.C. Haliburton's nineteenth-century satires of small-town Canadian life.

Look! The Land is Growing Giants is a localized legend based on the historical character of Joe Montferrand, the gentle lumber-boss whose strength, courage, and giant size became legendary in the Ottawa Valley in the nineteenth century. The combination of tall-tale narrative and poetic language creates an atmosphere of Canadian heroism. Richard Pelham's witty drawings complement the tone, which at times is ironic. Such details as the rollicking, poetic catalogues of Ottawa Valley place-names and the epic battle between Joe and the monstrous Windigo link this celebration of regional legend and humour with the mock-epic narrative poetry tradition exploited by Robert Service. Canadian heroes of legend and history are seldom ably interpreted for a child audience, but Finnigan's text—compared to the rougher treatment of the same character in the Paul Bunyanesque *Tall Tales of Joe Mufferaw* (1979) by Bernie Bedore—has a subtle heroism and poetic lyricism. It melds quasi-historical incident with character study and unites vivid mythic monsters with hyperbolic, impossible deeds. The legend concludes on a note of whimsical Canadian humour: Joe Montferrand sires a new race of indigenous giants that include the first Montreal Canadiens and future generations of hockey-players all across North America.

Jenni Lunn, who both retells and illustrates her Maritime version of *The Fisherman and His Wife*, sets the Grimm tale in a contemporary Nova Scotian fishing village. The vigorous dialect and salty, regional speech patterns give a freshness to the story-telling voice that recalls the recasting of Grimm tales in an English North Country dialect by the British folklorist Brian Alderson. Lunn highlights the Nova Scotia colloquialisms with touches of Maritime social satire; for example, the fisherman who becomes Chief Inspector for the Fisheries Department in order to satisfy his shrewish wife's pretensions spends his days eating ham sandwiches with his friends.

FOLKLORE OF ETHNIC GROUPS

The formal policy of multiculturalism announced by the federal government in the early 1970s brought new intonations to Canadian folklore that were different from aboriginal, French-Canadian, and Anglo-Canadian inflections. The diverse voices of ethnic minorities expressed their cultural values and immigrant experiences in folk materials that differed slightly from the earlier traditional bodies of lore. One group of folklore publications continues the tradition of retelling the familiar folktales of Europe or the Third World in a style that is relatively untouched by the Canadian environment or immigrant perception. Such is the case in two Ukrainian collections: *Fox Mykyta* (1978), vigorously illustrated by William Kurelek, which is the first English version of Ivan Franko's nineteenth-century Ukrainian allegory based on satirical Reynard the Fox trickster fables, and *The Flying Ship and Other Ukrainian Folk Tales* (1975), a rather pedestrian collection translated and retold by Victoria Symchych and Olga Vesey.

Other examples, such as the Kids Can Press 'Folktale Library' series of bilingual picture-book editions of international folklore, transmit the immigrant experience in a subtle way. The visual presentation of parallel texts in two languages—the language of origin and the English translation—suggests that cultural continuity is possible within the Canadian multicultural mosaic and that the folklore of all ethnic groups can enrich mainstream Canadian culture while retaining its own identity. That identity, which is tied into both the sound of a language and its visual appearance, is made concrete in the series by using the many calligraphic styles of the languages of origin. An effective melding of the text's calligraphy with the illustrator's choice of medium and artistic style is found in *Gonbei's Magic Kettle: A Folktale in Japanese and English* (1980), retold by Michiko Nakamura and illustrated by San Murata. The delicate, graceful characters of the Japanese calligraphy are a perfect complement to the pen-and-ink line-and-wash drawings. Both the calligraphy and the artwork—which recalls Japanese scroll paintings—echo the low-keyed wit and elegant simplicity of the story.

MATERIAL FOLKLORE

A country's folklore always includes a material, or non-verbal, folklore. Canadian publications for children often include elements of material folklore, such as arts and crafts, dance and music, popular customs and artifacts. Two examples are Michael Cutler's *Great Hockey Masks* (1983) and Carlo Italiano's *Sleighs: The Gentle Transportation* (1978; originally published under the title *The Sleighs of My Childhood*, 1974). Both books give a mythic dimension to objects of practical folkcraft; they also analyse their histories and folk variants. The author-artists' childlike fascination with observing and cataloguing physical artifacts shines through the adult nostalgia and memory in these folk-histories.

Another work that dramatizes an ancient folkcraft is Ulli Steltzer's *Building an Igloo* (1981), in which an Inuit father and son construct an igloo step-by-step out of snow in the old way, but with the help of a contemporary saw. The striking black-and-white photographs and spare text recall the photo-essay children's informational books on American folk art by Kathryn Lasky, such as *Dollmaker* (1981).

GAME LORE AND FOLK POETRY

Children's game lore is another form of universal folklore. It is accompanied by a vital oral folk poetry that provides rhythm and music for children's play: the cadences of nursery rhymes, street and game rhymes, riddles, tongue-twisters, wordplay, taunts, lullabies, and folksongs. Musical performance of this traditional children's poetry, both on stage and in the electronic media, has increased greatly in Canada in the last decade with the rise of popular singer-songwriters for children. Such Canadian troubadours as Raffi, Fred Penner, and the trio of Sharon, Lois, and Bram have moved beyond performance and recording to produce books of poetry, music, and song. The best of these is *Sharon, Lois and Bram's Mother Goose* (1985), a collection of traditional and contemporary verses with piano and guitar arrangements and playful, whimsical illustrations by Maryann Kovalski. Thematically structured, the cycle of 153 rhymes and songs, accompanied by innumerable drawings, chronicles a single day in the life of an exuberant family. The collection's full panoply of language and image resembles the richness of the classic *Mother Goose Treasury* (1966), a bumper collection robustly illustrated by British artist Raymond Briggs.

Turning from the folk poetry of the nursery, recited and sung by adults to pre-schoolers, to the private oral lore originating with, and transmitted by, the children's subculture, one sees Edith Fowke as Canada's answer to Britain's Peter and Iona Opie. Fowke has collected and edited two anthologies of Canadian children's street and game lore: *Sally Go Round the Sun: Three Hundred Songs, Rhymes and Games of Canadian Children* (1969) and *Ring Around the Moon: Two Hundred Songs, Tongue Twisters, Riddles and Rhymes of Canadian Children* (1977). These compilations of playground folk poetry, such as skipping rhymes, ball-bouncing chants, and game songs, offer a zesty introduction to the rich wordplay and brash energy of children's demotic language, as well as to the ongoing folk life of game lore.

While most of the lore and language are common to all English-language childhood, some elements are peculiar to Canada.

An intriguing addition to the field of game lore publications is Camilla Gryski's work on string-games: string figures woven on fingers by folk artists of primitive cultures who were often story-tellers. *Cat's Cradle, Owl's Eyes: A Book of String Games* (1983) and *Many Stars and More String Games* (1985) are companion books that give instructions for playing string games. They include information on the folklore of string and folktales from many cultures. In the country of origin these tales accompany the making of string patterns, much as the oral recital of street rhymes goes hand in hand with children's traditional playground games. Clear, practical, and direct, these unpretentious works dramatize the pattern-making function of the human mind. Patterns of mythic narrative come alive—physically through the magical string figures, and metaphorically, through the mirroring, parallel folktales.

A unique book that combines many of these elements of children's lore and language with general folk customs, song, and poetry is Alice Kane's *Songs and Sayings of an Ulster Childhood* (1983; edited by Edith Fowke). Shaped by the sensibility of a classic story-teller, it is an adult memoir of Kane's childhood in Belfast before and during the First World War. As well as offering English-language childhood lore, Kane documents the traditions and customs peculiar to her family and community. She paints an autobiographical portrait of a child growing up in an atmosphere of cultural continuity, in a large, loving family rich in oral language. In her family, song and poetry, proverbs and jokes are part of daily life, and every day is a part of living folklore. In the manner of earlier, discursive Victorian British country childhood memoirs, such as Flora Thompson's *Lark Rise to Candleford* (1945), Kane integrates the songs and sayings into an intimate narrative, creating social and community history out of her personal memories. She writes without self-consciousness, but with a profound sense of the immediacy of childhood perception. Her ability to recall the small, significant incidents that shape a child's emotional life and the specific words of song, poetry, and narrative that contribute to a child's sensitivity to language is impressive.

In a sense, *Songs and Sayings of an Ulster Childhood* demonstrates the transition of children's verse from the sensuous, rhythmic cadence and pungent humour found in early childhood oral poetry to the more subtle qualities of written poetry. The autobiography also gives an insight into the process whereby a child becomes a poet: little Alice, blessed by her immersion in the sea of vital, fresh language of a living oral culture, grows up to be Alice Kane, professional story-teller and writer, whose memoir sings with the musicality of poetry.

The diverse ingredients of the oral tradition—from folklore and mythology to oral poetry—simmer in the universal broth that fills what J.R.R. Tolkien has called the 'Cauldron of Story'. From its vital folk heritage Canada has derived a national lore that adds a unique seasoning to the richness of this ever-boiling cauldron.

ANDERSEN, LORRIE, IRENE AUBREY, AND LOUISE McDIARMID. *Storytellers' Rendezvous: Canadian Stories to Tell to Children*. Illustrations by Bo Kim Louie. Ottawa, Canadian Library Association, 1979, paper.

AUBREY, IRENE, LOUISE McDIARMID, AND LORRIE ANDERSEN, comps. *Storytellers' Encore: More Canadian Stories to Tell to Children*. Ottawa, Canadian Library Association, 1984, paper.

AUBRY, CLAUDE. *The Magic Fiddler and Other Legends of French Canada*. Translated by Alice E. Kane. Graphics by Saul Field. Toronto, Martin, 1968, cloth (O.P.), paper.

AYRE, ROBERT. *Sketco the Raven*. Illustrated by Philip Surrey. Toronto, Macmillan, 1961, cloth (O.P.)

BARBEAU, MARIUS. *The Golden Phoenix, and Other French-Canadian Fairy Tales*. Retold by Michael Hornyansky. Illustrated by Arthur Price. Toronto, Oxford, 1958, cloth (O.P.); Reprinted under title: *The Golden Phoenix, and Other Fairy Tales from Quebec*. 1980, paper.

BEDORE, BERNIE. *Tall Tales of Joe Mufferaw*. Designed and illustrated by Yüksel Hassan. Toronto, Consolidated Amethyst, 1979, paper (Folklore Series)

CAMERON, ANNE. *How Raven Freed the Moon*. Illustrations by Tara Miller. Madeira Park, B.C., Harbour, 1985, paper.

CAMPBELL, MARIA. *Little Badger and the Fire Spirit*. Illustrated by David Maclagan. Toronto, M & S, 1977, cloth (O.P.)

CLUTESI, GEORGE. *Son of Raven, Son of Deer: Fables of the Tse-Shaht People*. Illustrated by the author. Sidney, B.C., Gray's, 1967, cloth (O.P.); 1975, paper.

COATSWORTH, EMERSON AND DAVID COATSWORTH, comps. *The Adventures of Nanabush: Ojibway Indian Stories*. Told by Sam Snake, Chief Elijah Yellowhead, Alder York, David Simcoe, and Annie King. Illustrated by Francis Kagige. Toronto, Doubleday, 1979, cloth, paper.

COLOMBO, JOHN ROBERT, ed. *Poems of the Inuit*. Ottawa, Oberon, 1981, cloth.

CUTLER, MICHAEL M.. *Hockey Masks and the Great Goalies Who Wore Them*. Paintings by the author. Montreal, Tundra, 1977, paper; Rev. edn under title: *Great Hockey Masks*. Illustrated by the author. 1983, paper.

DOWNIE, MARY ALICE. *The Wicked Fairy-Wife: A French Canadian Folktale*. Translated and adapted from the French. Illustrated by Kim Price. Toronto, Kids Can, 1983, paper.

_____. *The Witch of the North: Folk Tales of French Canada*. Collages by Elizabeth Cleaver. Ottawa, Oberon, 1975, cloth (O.P.)

FINNIGAN, JOAN. *Look! The Land is Growing Giants: A Very Canadian Legend*. Drawings by Richard Pelham. Montreal, Tundra, 1983, cloth.

FOWKE, EDITH. *Folklore of Canada*. Illustrations by Laszlo Gal. Toronto, M & S, 1976, cloth (O.P.), paper.

_____. *Folktales of French Canada*. Illustrations by Henri Julien. Toronto, NC Press, 1979, paper; Rev. edn, 1981, paper; New edn, 1982, paper.

_____. *Ring Around the Moon*. Illustrated by Judith Gwyn Brown. Toronto, M & S, 1977, cloth (O.P.)

_____. *Sally Go Round the Sun: 300 Songs, Rhymes and Games of Canadian Children*. Musical Arrangements by Keith MacMillan. Illustrated by Carlos Marchiori. Designed by Frank Newfeld and Don Fernley. Toronto/Montreal, M & S, 1969, cloth.

FRANKO, IVAN. *Fox Mykyta*. English version by Bohdan Melnyk. Illustrated by William Kurelek. Montreal, Tundra, 1978, cloth.

GRYSKI, CAMILLA. *Cat's Cradle, Owl's Eyes: A Book of String Games*. Illustrated by Tom Sankey, Toronto, Kids Can, 1983, paper.

_____. *Many Stars and More String Games*. Illustrated by Tom Sankey. Toronto, Kids Can, 1985, cloth, paper.

HAMILTON, MARY. *A New World Bestiary*. Illustrated by Kim La Fave. Vancouver/Toronto, Douglas, 1985, cloth.

HARRIS, CHRISTIE. *Mouse Woman and the Mischief-Makers*. Drawings by Douglas Tait. Toronto, M & S, 1977, cloth; 1984, paper (Canadian Favourites)

_____. *Mouse Woman and the Muddleheads*. Drawings by Douglas Tait. Toronto, M & S, 1979, cloth.

_____. *Mouse Woman and the Vanished Princesses*. Drawings by Douglas Tait. Toronto, M & S, 1976, cloth.

_____. *Once Upon a Totem*. Woodcuts by John Frazer Mills. Toronto, M & S, 1963, cloth (O.P.); 1978, paper (Canadian Favourites)

_____. *The Trouble with Adventurers*. Drawings by Douglas Tait. Toronto, M & S, 1982, cloth.

_____. *The Trouble with Princesses*. Drawings by Douglas Tait. Toronto, M & S, 1980, cloth (O.P.); 1984, paper (Canadian Favourites) (O.P.)

HEWITT, GARNET. *Ytek and the Arctic Orchid: An Inuit Legend*. Illustrations by Heather Woodall. Vancouver/Toronto, Douglas, 1981, cloth (O.P.); 1983, paper.

HOUSTON, JAMES. *Kiviok's Magic Journey: An Eskimo Legend*. Illustrated by the author. Don Mills, Ont., Longman, 1973, cloth (O.P.)

_____. *Songs of the Dream People: Chants and Images from the Indians and Eskimos of North America*. Illustrated by James Houston. Don Mills, Ont., Longman, 1972, cloth, (O.P.)

ITALIANO, CARLO. *The Sleighs of My Childhood/Les Traîneaux de Mon Enfance*. Translated by René Chicoine. Illustrated by the author. Montreal, Tundra, 1974, cloth (O.P.); Reprinted under title: *Sleighs: The Gentle Transportation*. Montreal/New York, Tundra, 1978, cloth, paper.

JOHNSON, EMILY PAULINE. *Legends of Vancouver*. Illustrated by Ben Lim. New edn Toronto, M & S , 1961, paper. (Originally published in 1911 in a privately printed edition.)

JOHNSTON, BASIL H. *Tales the Elders Told: Ojibway Legends*. Paintings and drawings by Shirley Cheechoo. Toronto, Royal Ontario Museum, 1981, cloth.

KANE, ALICE. *Songs and Sayings of an Ulster Childhood*. Edited by Edith Fowke. Toronto, M & S, 1983, cloth.

LEWIS, RICHARD, ed. *I Breathe a New Song: Poems of the Eskimo*. Illustrated by Oonark. Introduction by Edmund Carpenter. New York, Simon, 1971, cloth (O.P.)

LUNN, JENNI. *The Fisherman and His Wife: A Grimm's Fairytale*. Illustrated by the author. Toronto/Montreal/New York, McGraw, 1982, cloth (O.P.)

MACKLEM, MICHAEL. *Jacques the Woodcutter*. Illustrations by Ann Blades. Ottawa, Oberon, 1977, cloth (O.P.)

MACMILLAN, CYRUS. *Canadian Wonder Tales*. Illustrated by George Sheringham. London, Lane, 1918, cloth (O.P.); Reissued, with *Canadian Fairy Tales*, under title: *Canadian Wonder Tales*. Illustrated by Elizabeth Cleaver, Toronto, Clarke, 1974, cloth (O.P.)

MARKOOSIE. *Harpoon of the Hunter*. Illustrations by Germaine Arnaktauyok. Montreal/London, McGill-Queen's, 1970, cloth, paper.

MARTIN, EVA. *Canadian Fairy Tales*. Illustrated by Laszlo Gal. Vancouver/Toronto, Douglas, 1984, cloth (O.P.), paper (A Groundwood Book)

MELZACK, RONALD. *Why the Man in the Moon is Happy and Other Eskimo Creation Stories*. Illustrated by Laszlo Gal. Toronto, M & S, 1977, cloth (O.P.)

METAYER, MAURICE. *Tales from the Igloo*. Foreword by Al Purdy. Illustrated by Agnes Nanogak. Edmonton, Hurtig, 1972, cloth (O.P.), paper.

MOTHER GOOSE. *Sharon, Lois and Bram's Mother Goose*. Illustrated by Maryann Kovalski. Vancouver/Toronto, Douglas, 1985, paper.

NAKAMURA, MICHIKO. *Gonbei's Magic Kettle: A Folktale in Japanese and English*. Illustrated by San Murata. Calligraphy by Banri Nakamura. Toronto, Kids Can, 1980, paper (Folktale Library)

NOWLAN, ALDEN. *Nine Micmac Legends*. Illustrated by Shirley Bear. Hantsport, N.S., Lancelot, 1983, paper.

REID, BILL AND ROBERT BRINGHURST. *The Raven Steals the Light*. Drawings by Bill Reid. Vancouver/Toronto, Douglas, 1984, cloth.

ROBINSON, GAIL. *Raven the Trickster: Legends of the North American Indians*. Introduced by Douglas Hill. Illustrated by Joanna Troughton. Toronto, Clarke, 1981, cloth (O.P.)

SCRIBE, MURDO. *Murdo's Story: A Legend from Northern Manitoba*. Illustrated by Terry Gallagher. Winnipeg, Pemmican, 1985, paper.

SKOGAN, JOAN. *The Princess and the Sea-Bear and Other Tsimshian Stories*. Illustrations by Claudia Stewart. Prince Rupert, B.C., Metlakatla Band Council, 1983, paper (O.P.)

SPRAY, CAROLE. *The Mare's Egg: A New World Folk Tale*. Afterword by Margaret Atwood. Illustrated by Kim La Fave. Camden East, Ont., Camden, 1981, cloth, paper.

STELTZER, ULLI. *Building an Igloo*. Photographs by the author. Vancouver, Douglas, 1981, cloth.

STORIES FROM PANGNIRTUNG. Illustrated by Germaine Arnaktauyok. Foreword by Stuart Hodgson. Edmonton, Hurtig, 1976, cloth (O.P.)

SYMCHYCH, VICTORIA AND OLGA VESEY. *The Flying Ship and Other Ukrainian Folk Tales*. Illustrated by Peter Kuch. Toronto/Montreal, Holt, 1975, cloth.

TROENDLE, YVES. *Raven's Children: A Novel Based on the Myths of the Northwest Coast Indians*. Illustrations by Raymond Verdaguer. Lantzville, B.C., Oolichan, 1979, cloth, paper.

5

POETRY

Compared to other genres of children's literature, Canadian poetry for children has been late in developing; there are still few poets of any real substance or significance. This slow growth reflects an international trend; children's poetry continued to follow the didactic and the doggerel verse traditions long after children's fiction had evolved into real literature.

In the early twentieth century many Canadian poetic works for adults were appropriated for children, such as Pauline Johnson's *Flint and Feather* (1912). Children enjoyed Johnson's clear and lyrical nature poetry and narrative verse, which reflected the Canadian landscape and native life. Unfortunately, other early Canadian poets, such as Isabel Eccleston Mackay, who wrote specifically for children, produced sentimental and patronizing verse.

NONSENSE AND DOMESTIC POETRY

Contemporary Canadian children's poets are primarily writers of nonsense verse. They reflect an international trend in which most of the poetry created for children is vigorous, lighthearted doggerel. Few of these poets display the sense of nuance or the subtlety of Walter de la Mare, for example, but they do create moments of musicality and flashes of verbal wit and wordplay. Most Canadian poets for children write popular light verse for the pre-schooler and early elementary-school child that is similar to the works of the Americans Shel Silverstein and Jack Prelutsky; few of them are exploring the poetic traditions of mature, contemplative lyric or nature poetry, as America's David McCord and England's Ted Hughes are doing in their children's verse.

The most popular children's poet in Canada is Dennis Lee. His poetry—predominantly nonsense verse that includes domestic, narrative, and lyric elements—is written with a crafted simplicity. Its roots are the oral traditions of early childhood literature: the lullabies, nursery rhymes, and action verses that accompany fingerplays, dandling games, and the tickling of babies; and the incantatory rhymes, chants, and taunts of children's street and game lore. The metrical cadences of Lee's rhythms are like those heard in Mother Goose, Robert Louis Stevenson, and A.A. Milne: the basic, repetitive, pounding beat and compelling, satisfying rhyme of traditional children's verse. These sound patterns, which are fundamental, make Lee's poetry come alive when read aloud.

Like Stevenson and Milne, Lee observes closely the self-absorbed, inner life of the very young. His intermittent use of a child-narrator's point of view emphasizes the importance of friendship and play, of imagination and emotion. The warmth of Lee's domestic poems is counterpointed by the wild, anarchic spirit of his nonsense verse, which breaks parental social taboos and behavioural codes, explores children's primal fantasies, and flirts with the forbidden and the risqué. Lee's language—his indefatigable jumbling of puns, tongue-twisters, and invented words, his frenetic visions of the absurd—creates a subversive subtext to his seemingly simple verse.

At times Lee's nonsense is banal and his focus on childhood fascination with mild scatology can be tasteless, but, on the whole, he supplies a healthy, imaginative release in creative play. The act of reversal, of making nonsense, can clarify meaning and establish structure and sense in a child's perception of life and language patterns.

In all his works, from his first poetry collections (*Alligator Pie*, 1974; *Nicholas Knock and Other People*, 1974; *Garbage Delight*, 1977) to his most recent (*Jelly Belly*, 1983), Lee's domestic and nonsense verse exhibit a wistful, transparent lyricism, a sense of unity with the world, and a recognition of emotional truths. As well as mapping a child's emotional geography, Lee delineates Canada's urban landscape. His poems are rich in allusions to skyscrapers and laundromats, and his images are consciously and uniquely Canadian: they include place names (from Chicoutimi to Mississauga), historical characters (William Lyon Mackenzie King), and national pastimes (in a parody of a Milne poem, a unique hockey game is played by a worm, a flea, an elephant, and a bore). None of these details are self-consciously patriotic; the Canadian words and images are transformed into incantatory tongue-twisters and onomatopoeic talismans and charms. In the magical recital of these emblems of Canadian culture, Moose Jaw becomes as mythic as Banbury Cross. Lee has been dubbed Canada's Father Goose; children who enjoy his poetry will certainly absorb the inflections of a Canadian sensibility, of a folklore poetics grounded in a real time and place and as evocative as Mother Goose's legendary kingdom.

The illustrators of Lee's verse have approached his poetic vision from various perspectives. Frank Newfeld interprets the rhymes of *Alligator Pie*, *Nicholas Knock and Other People*, and *Garbage Delight* in a series of brightly animated, crisp vignettes. Unfortunately, Newfeld's art has a stiff formality that does not fully complement the elasticity of Lee's writing.

Jelly Belly is illustrated by Juan Wijngaard, who resides in England. Wjingaard's delicately muted, pastel-toned drawings have an air of magic realism that suggests the vision of a contemporary Arthur Rackham and gives the rhymes the folk charm of an updated Mother Goose. Details of clothing, architecture, and locale are more urban British than Canadian. The sketches dramatize Lee's blending of the child's imaginary fantasies with scenes from the real world; motifs, such as the figure of the ogrish Jelly Belly, reappear from page to page, first as a raging folk-monster of the mind, and later as a harmless toy mural in a child's room. This visual interplay with the poems explores the child's inner life, where the wit and humour of nonsense fantasies help to heal the pains of rage, fear, and anxiety. Glorious, loony silliness subtly defuses turbulent emotions.

This also occurs in Lee's single-illustrated poem *Lizzie's Lion* (1984), a mock cautionary tale in verse in the rather black-humoured poetic tradition of Heinrich Hoffman's *Struwwelpeter* (1848) and Hilaire Belloc's *Cautionary Tales for Children* (1918). The jaunty metre and rhyme and the exaggerated zest with which a young girl's watch-dog lion devours a wicked robber are also related to the satirical parodies found in Tomi Ungerer's picture-books. As in Ungerer's illustrations, the decidedly non-naturalistic, zany pictures by Marie-Louise Gay tend to distance the reader from the literary violence.

Lizzy's Lion is representative of the international trend towards publishing picture-books with rhyming texts. These single-poem picture-books are a companion form to the ubiquitous single-illustrated folk-tales. Canadian examples range from the re-illustration of classic poems, such as Ron Berg's decorative, Edwardian-style version of Edward Lear's *The Owl and the Pussycat* (1984), to contemporary lullabies and nursery verse for pre-schoolers, which are marked by melodic and rhythmic language, and the simplest of stories, such as bp Nichol's soothing animal bedtime rhyme, *Once: A Lullaby* (1983; illustrated by Ed Roach).

A standard lullaby for a picture-book text is a classic nineteenth-century verse from the American children's poet Eugene Field. The illustrations by Ron Berg for Field's *Wynken, Blynken and Nod* (1985) are soft representational drawings in dreamy, muted tones. Berg uses a visual frame-device; the comforting ritual of the bedtime story is stressed in the pictures of a father (whose face is echoed in the benign visage of the man-in-the moon) reading to his daughter and tucking her into bed after the girl's imaginary, exhilarating flight through the night sky with her toy rabbit and teddy-bear. The child and her toys become the three characters in the fantasy-dream poem.

A more volatile side of the parent-child relationship is the subject of two spirited picture-book poems: Sue Ann Alderson's coupling of free verse and rhyming refrain in *Bonnie McSmithers, You're Driving Me Dithers* (1974) and Phoebe Gilman's rhyming couplets in *Jillian Jiggs* (1985). In both texts a cumulative, hypnotic effect is produced by recurring refrains as a mother's lament at her daughter's antics shifts from irritation to frenzy and, finally, to gentle acceptance. These turbulent and good-humoured developments are echoed in the wit of the illustrations. The artwork for each book could not be more different. Fiona Garrick's black-and-white pen drawings for *Bonnie McSmithers, You're Driving Me Dithers* are stylized and static, while Phoebe Gilman's colourful, modified cartoon sketches for *Jillian Jiggs* are dynamic with movement. Gilman's drawings literally overflow the picture frames and extend the verse narrative with a separate story—an endearing visual commentary on the younger, tag-along sister's play. Both artists stress the domestic humour in the relationship between a creative, messy child and a distracted, loving mother.

The domestic poetry sub-genre also includes more mature verse that explores the family, the school, and the inner lives of primary-grade children. Following Lee's example in combining domestic and nonsense verse with Canadian subjects and themes are two collections for the school-aged child: Robert Heidbreder's *Don't Eat Spiders* (1985) and Lois Simmie's *Auntie's Knitting a Baby* (1984).

Heidbreder's poems are designed for oral recital and group involvement, both in the classroom and on the playground. His verse is similar to Lee's colloquial rhymes and to the oral stories of Robert Munsch. The natural speaking voice, catchy rhythms, musical sound patterns, and the subjects of children's ordinary life—clowns, robots, spiders—render the poems immediately accessible. The empathy with children and the irreverent energy that mark Lee's success are also present in *Don't Eat Spiders*, and are extended through Karen Patkau's blazingly coloured, tactile collages. Heidbreder's nonsense has a raw vigour and his nature poetry exhibits a lyrical quality reminiscent of haiku. And, like both Lee and Lois Simmie, Heidbreder combines nonsensical and fantastical creatures with Canadian motifs and places: he tells of a dragon in the Casa Loma tower, and, in 'Sticky Maple Syrup', propels a national symbol into an ironically humorous Canadian folk dimension.

A more sophisticated poet for intermediate readers is Lois Simmie, who also blends light verse with domestic poetry. Her poetic voice is less jaunty and robust, more subtle and ironic than either Lee or Heidbreder. Several poem cycles on various themes are interwoven throughout the book, creating a pattern of recurring images, characters, puns, and running gags, from the terrible fate awaiting Mary McBickle who repeatedly chokes on a pickle to the unnatural shapes evolving from Auntie's knitting of a baby-bonnet. Simmie absorbs her crafted, figurative language into a colloquial style. Her controlled rhythms and rhymes suggest the audacity of Ogden Nash's nonsense or of David McCord's light wordplay. There is also a reflective poignancy in Simmie's poems of emotional change in a child's world and there is a wistfulness in her nonsense creatures, which are reminiscent of Edward Lear's touching creations; these elements show Simmie's sensitivity not only to the vulnerability and delicacy of children's inner imaginations but to the gritty naturalism of their daily lives.

Lee, Heidbreder, and Simmie share an intuitive understanding of the nature of nonsense poetry. Like Edward Lear and Lewis Caroll, they understand that order and logic are needed to create convincing nonsense and that there is a fine line between gentle irony and bleak satire, between fantastical light verse and harsh surrealism. This crucial precision and balance are not achieved by Irving Layton and sean o huigin in their nonsense poetry for children. Layton's evocative imagery and subtle metre in *A Spider Danced a Cosy Jig* (1984) give his work an arresting figurative and musical presence, but the misanthropic parodies of human behaviour in these poems of animal beauty and suffering and Layton's cynical vision betray the work's true spirit: it is adult social satire rather than children's nonsense or nature poetry.

sean o huigin shows an inventive use of experimental verse forms, such as concrete, sound, and visual poetry. His long free-verse, colloquial poems, which abandon the conventions of punctuation and capitalization, are unusual in the traditionally conservative field of children's poetry. Though his concepts are often original and inventive, as in the two-track, extended poem of a nightmare double life, *Blink: A Strange Poem for Children* (1984), his prolific output is highly uneven. Many poems are marred by moments of arbitrary formlessness and heavy-handed didacticism. Of course, iconoclastic parodies and nonsense reversals that poke fun at adult society have tremendous appeal to children, who are also fascinated by the bizarre and the taboo and enjoy being titillated by their own fears and fantasies. For younger children, Heidbreder tempers these irresistible images of nightmare with a bright, sunny wit. But o huigin's cautionary gothic horrors for older children in *Scary Poems for Rotten Kids* (1982) and *The Dinner Party* (1984) seem to go over the edge into gratuitous violence and grotesque fear, especially when compared to the American Jack Prelutsky's classic work on the same theme of monsters of the mind, *Nightmares: Poems to Trouble Your Sleep* (1976).

NARRATIVE, NATURE, AND LYRIC POETRY

A more successful work by o huigin is his long, narrative free-verse poem, *The Ghost Horse of the Mounties* (1983). Based on a historical incident in the early days of the Northwest Mounted Police—a summer lightning storm and a horse stampede at Dufferin, Manitoba in 1874—this epic story-poem is suffused with romantic lyricism. Figurative language and onomatopoeic rhythm evoke the night of storm, the violent stampede, and the odyssey of the ghost horse; o huigin makes palpable the dramatic atmosphere of the bare, dark prairie under attack by a dreadful storm, as well as the pathos and the supernatural elements in the undying love between a young man and his horse. The result is a work of romantic tragedy and folk heroism in the style of pioneer folk songs and ballads, such as 'John Henry'.

The Ghost Horse of the Mounties also conveys a vivid sense of landscape: the desolate prairie, with its natural beauty and wild storms. And, in an innovative device, the poem employs three voices: the incantatory voice of the bardic narrator and the interior monologues of the young mountie and his horse. The reader is urged to empathize imaginatively with both the young man and the horse, and to participate in the creation of character and drama. This is a kind of nature poetry in which the prairie and the lost horse become not only powerful symbols but very real characters.

Considering the impact of the Canadian landscape on children's fiction, it is surprising that nature poetry written specifically for children—poems of the seasons, of plant and animal life, of Canada's physical geography—has been rare and, usually, mediocre. Despite the strengths of Canadian adult poetry in this area, there is no poet of the calibre of Ted Hughes in England or Harry Behn in the United States who is celebrating the natural world for children in Canada. Robert Heidbreder's nature lyrics possess a gentle music, and there is clarity and precision in George Swede's haiku in *Tick Bird: Poems for Children* (1983) and *Time is Flies: Poems for Children* (1984). But for truly evocative nature verse, as well as for mature lyric poetry, one must turn to Canadian adult poetry selected for children.

Many of Dennis Lee's narrative and lyric poems for older children in *Nicholas Knock and Other People* have a philosophical and thought-provoking quality, but no other children's collection has appeared in the last decade to equal it. Since 1975, the most powerful collection of contemplative poetry for older children and teenagers is Raymond Souster's *Flight of the Roller-Coaster: Poems for Younger Readers* (1985), composed of works originally written for adults. Whether Souster's brief lyrics evoke the hockey games of his childhood or observe a morning-glory or his cat, the writing has the clear imagery, intense emotion, and musicality of the best poetry for children. The tendency in international publishing to select poems from an adult poet's body of work as a means of introducing children to adult poetry has resulted in many strong collections, including Langston Hughes's *Don't You Turn Back* (1969) and Robert Frost's *You Come Too* (1959). Like Hughes and Frost, Souster uses an intimate, colloquial voice in his luminous poems about the unity of existence in daily life.

As well as selected introductions to single adult poets, a common staple of publishing is the broader anthology—the compilation of a range of adult poetry selected for children on a theme or genre, or from a national perspective. The best poetry anthologies for children may be classic works selected from adult writing by sensitive editors who are also poets, such as Walter de la Mare in *Come Hither* (1922) or Seamus Heaney and Ted Hughes in *The Rattle Bag* (1982). A fine example of this approach in Canada is Mary Alice Downie and Barbara Robertson's *The New Wind Has Wings: Poems From Canada* (1984, the revised edition of *The Wind Has Wings: Poems from Canada*, 1968). The compilers have chosen Canadian adult poetry with appeal to children, including traditional folk and aboriginal poetry, and a balanced selection from classic and contemporary poets, from Bliss Carman, Robert Service, and Pauline Johnson to E.J. Pratt, Frank Davey, and P.K. Page. The selections share the immediacy of a child's vision, especially in the many nature poems. Strong, somewhat abstract illustrations by Elizabeth Cleaver suggestively complement the word-pictures of the poems.

WRITING BY CHILDREN

Another group of anthologies offers poetry written by children. The American Richard Lewis pioneered the compilation of children's creative writing with his editing of the seminal *Miracles: Poems by Children of the English-speaking World* (1966). Poets, critics, and teachers, such as Myra Cohn Livingston and Kenneth Koch, have disagreed on the concept of the child as poet. Despite some reservations about the literary and artistic value of poetry written by children and some questions about whether such works are of more interest to adults than to children, collections of Canadian children's poetry do provide examples of children's ability to use language freshly and inventively. The anthologies also open a window on the thoughts, emotions, and imaginations of Canadian children. In the early 1970s publishers devoted solely to publishing writing and art by children—for example, Books by Kids, which became Annick Press—produced works such as *Wordsandwich* (1975). In the last decade collections of this sort have proliferated beyond measure.

One of the subjects most often addressed in the poetry written by the young is their delight in nature. Lyrics revealing a deep kinship with, and a respect for, the natural world are certainly central to Sean Ferris's *Children of the Great Muskeg* (1985), a compilation of poems and artwork by Cree and Métis children living in Northern Ontario. The children's black-and-white and colour drawings exhibit a sense of traditional native design. The unpretentious free-verse poetry reveals a passionate love for the subarctic land, a sympathy for the wildlife, and an elegiac lyricism about the loss of the native heritage. Most poems reflect the conflict between old and new traditions; images of contemporary life—ski-doos, guns, television, and alcohol—are juxtaposed with those of surviving folk customs and mythic creatures, such as hunting rituals and the fearsome Windigo.

Canadian poets for adults have used images from native myth and legend, but poets for children have rarely done so. Their work is more urban and contemporary. But it is natural for aboriginal mythic image and lore to appear in poetry by native children. This material has also been treated in the form of legends retold by Indian children of British Columbia in a work published before 1975, *Tales from the Longhouse* (1973). Like *Children of the Great Muskeg*, this work is a blend of contemporary customs and traditional lore, and, although it is not poetry, it displays a poetic conviction.

Quite different from these visions of nature and myth is the social realism expressed by the urban, immigrant children in *Come with Us: Children Speak for Themselves* (1978). The accounts of these children form snapshot images of our multicultural society: memories of the original homelands and arrival in Canada; conflicts and discoveries in city streets, at school, and at work; problems with language, culture, identity, and racism; and the comfort of friendship and family love. The selections include primarily prose pieces, with some free-verse poetry, but the stories are most often expressed in a prose made poetic by its simplicity. The children's voices in these anthologies—honest and intensely emotional—remind us of the twin roots of all Canadian children's literature: aboriginal life and the immigrant experience.

The poetic tradition in Canadian adult writing has always been a strong force in Canadian literature. And ever since the publication of *Alligator Pie* in 1974 Canadian children's poetry has been gaining in stature and scope. This book of joyous poetry became the harbinger of a new era, perhaps because it was created—unlike the more private mode of fiction—for communal participation. It showed a national audience of adult and child readers, writers, and publishers that a Canadian children's mythology of place, history, and daily life already existed, and that it could be named and owned through the creative play of imaginative language and humour.

ALDERSON, SUE ANN. *Bonnie McSmithers, You're Driving Me Dithers*. Illustrations by Fiona Garrick. Edmonton, Tree Frog, 1974, cloth (O.P.), paper.

B.C. INDIAN ARTS SOCIETY. *Tales from the Longhouse*. By Indian Children of British Columbia. Sidney, B.C., Gray's, 1973, cloth (O.P.), paper.

DOWNIE, MARY ALICE AND BARBARA ROBERTSON, comps. *The New Wind Has Wings: Poems from Canada*. Illustrated by Elizabeth Cleaver. Toronto, Oxford, 1984, cloth, paper.

_____. *The Wind Has Wings: Poems from Canada*. Illustrated by Elizabeth Cleaver. Toronto, Oxford, 1968, cloth (O.P.); 1978, paper (O.P.), Rev. edn under title: *The New Wind Has Wings: Poems from Canada*. 1984, cloth, paper.

FERRIS, SEAN. *Children of the Great Muskeg*. Windsor, Ont., Black Moss, 1985, paper (O.P.)

FIELD, EUGENE. *Wynken, Blynken and Nod*. Illustrated by Ron Berg. Richmond Hill, Ont., North Winds, 1985, cloth, paper.

GILMAN, PHOEBE. *Jillian Jiggs*. Illustrated by the author. Richmond Hill, Ont., North Winds, 1985, cloth, paper.

HEIDBREDER, ROBERT. *Don't Eat Spiders*. Pictures by Karen Patkau. Toronto, Oxford, 1985, cloth.

JOHNSON, EMILY PAULINE. *Flint and Feather*. Toronto, Musson, 1912, cloth (O.P.)

LAYTON, IRVING. *A Spider Danced a Cosy Jig*. Edited by Elspeth Cameron. Illustrations by Miro Malish. Toronto, Stoddart, 1984, cloth.

LEAR, EDWARD. *The Owl and the Pussycast*. Illustrated by Ron Berg. Richmond Hill, Ont., North Winds, 1984, cloth, paper.

LEE, DENNIS. *Alligator Pie*. Pictures by Frank Newfeld. Toronto, Macmillan, 1974, cloth.

_____. *Garbage Delight*. Pictures by Frank Newfeld. Toronto, Macmillan, 1977, cloth.

_____. *Jelly Belly*. Illustrated by Juan Wijngaard. Toronto, Macmillan, 1983, cloth.

_____. *Lizzy's Lion*. Illustrated by Marie-Louise Gay. Toronto, Stoddart, 1984, cloth.

_____. *Nicholas Knock and Other People*. Pictures by Frank Newfeld. Toronto, Macmillan, 1974, cloth (O.P.)

MCCLARD, JUDY AND NAOMI WALL, eds. *Come With Us: Children Speak for Themselves*. Toronto, Women's Educational Press, 1978, paper.

NICHOL, BP. *Once: A Lullaby*. Illustrations by Ed Roach. Windsor, Ont., Black Moss, 1983, cloth, paper

O HUIGIN, SEAN. *Blink: (A Strange Book for Children)*. Pictures by Barbara Di Lella. Windsor, Ont., Black Moss, 1984, paper (O.P.)

_____. *The Dinner Party*. Illustrations by Maureen Paxton, Windsor, Ont., Black Moss, 1984, paper.

_____. *The Ghost Horse of the Mounties*. Designed and illustrated by Phil McLeod. Windsor, Ont., Black Moss, 1983, paper (O.P.)

_____. *Scary Poems for Rotten Kids*. Illustrations by Anthony Le Baron. Windsor, Ont., Black Moss, 1982, paper.

SIMMIE, LOIS. *Auntie's Knitting a Baby*. Illustrated by Anne Simmie. Saskatoon, Sask., Western, 1984, cloth, paper.

SOUSTER, RAYMOND. *Flight of the Roller-Coaster: Poems for Younger Readers*. Selected by Richard Woollatt. Ottawa, Oberon, 1985, paper.

SWEDE, GEORGE. *Tick Bird: Poems for Children*. Illustrations by Katherine Helmer. Toronto, Three Trees, 1983, cloth, paper.

_____. *Time Is Flies: Poems for Children*. Illustrations by Darcia Labrosse. Toronto, Three Trees, 1984, cloth, paper.

WORDSANDWICH. Toronto, Books by Kids, 1975, paper (O.P.)

CONCLUSION

Canadian children's books now form a loose confederation of shared national literary confidence, even though their differences reflect the vastness and variety of the land itself. Some of the new books possess a distinctive national character and flavour, taking their subject matter from what is unique in the Canadian experience. Others echo the themes and motifs found in adult Canadian writing.

Like their counterparts writing for adults, many Canadian writers for children have succeeded in mythologizing the landscape, although their cultural outlook is, on the whole, less oblique, distanced, and gloomy. Child and adolescent protagonists in Canadian children's books may struggle for physical or psychological survival, exist in isolation or alienation, but they are rarely victims. They are active participants in the unfolding drama of Canadian legend, history, and present-day life. In these books children grow to respect the natural world and to appreciate the Canadian cultural heritage; they become rooted in living tradition. Other Canadian children's writers give local coloration to universal childhood experience, aligning themselves with the trends and patterns of international children's literature. But, like all literature, children's books have a wide reach: the best of the books that interpret Canadian life and values also tell us about ourselves as members of the human community.

While the early 1970s to the present has been the most exhilarating and energetic period in Canadian children's literature to date—a time of new beginnings and the emergence of new traditions, rivalled only by the earlier, quite different era of Seton, Roberts, and Montgomery—publishing remains a risky business, and the literature still faces tremendous difficulties. Some of these have been, or are in the process of being, resolved. But unlimited perseverance and creative energy are still required if the commitment, the momentum, and the successes of the last decade are to continue. We cannot foretell the future, but it is reasonable to expect that the labours of 1975 to 1985, which brought the literature from an embryonic state to the threshold of maturity, must surely bear fruit that will enrich our culture even further.

INDEX

(AUTHORS, TITLES, ILLUSTRATORS)